# PSYCHIC ROOTS

*Serendipity & Intuition
in Genealogy*

# PSYCHIC ROOTS

## *Serendipity & Intuition in Genealogy*

**Henry Z Jones, Jr.**

Fellow of the American
Society of Genealogists

Published by Genealogical Publishing Co., Inc.
1001 N. Calvert St., Baltimore, MD 21202
Second printing 1994
Third printing 1995
Fourth printing 1996
Fifth printing 1997
Library of Congress Catalogue Card Number 93-78363
International Standard Book Number 0-8063-1388-9
*Made in the United States of America*

Extracts from the following works have been used with the
permission of the authors or publishers:

Book review by Jane Fletcher Fiske in *The New England Historical and
Genealogical Register*, Vol. CXLIV, July 1990.

*Incredible Coincidence: The Baffling World of Synchronicity*, by
Alan Vaughan (New York: Ballantine Books).

Five stories from the "Relatively Speaking" column in *Everton's
Genealogical Helper* (Nibley, Utah: Everton Publishers).

*The Roots of Coincidence*, by Arthur Koestler (New York: Vintage Books).

"Books with a Past," by Helen S. Ullmann, *Ensign* (February 1991).

WITH APPRECIATION TO

MY FRIENDS & COLLEAGUES

WHO DARED TO SHARE

THEIR EXPERIENCES

# CONTENTS

# ILLUSTRATIONS

# FOREWORD
## by Helen Hinchliff, Ph.D.

In 1983, in honor of my recent discovery of genealogy, my brother, Timothy Hinchliff, made a yarn painting for me entitled *Old Soul*. Without really knowing a genealogist's sources or methods, Tim used thousands of colored threads to depict his view that I am a sojourner between the living and the dead. Coincidentally, the picture captured the essence of this book. In the lower left corner, lighting my path with magic crystals is Old Soul, most easily imagined as a friendly white ghost. In the center are my ancestors, ranged in a circle. They are connected by a mysterious umbilical cord to Old Soul and to a second circle composed of my living relatives who reside in the upper right corner. Guided by Old Soul, I travel a path between them, learning from each, communing with each.

Many of the contributors to this book know of Old Soul, although they might call Him by another name: within these pages you will encounter the Great God of Genealogy, fate, Providence, God. Regardless of the name that is used, all who sense this force report that it empowers them to get in touch with and to learn from their ancestors.

Others report no overarching force at work on their behalf; however, some point to ancestors who have beckoned to them, led them, or otherwise made their presence known. It appears that untold numbers of ancestors have asked to be understood and to have their stories told, fully and accurately. They call to us so  persistently and with such apparent feeling that we who hear their pleas are motivated to cast aside all other pursuits to do their bidding. Perhaps Hank Jones expresses this phenomenon best when describing his love affair with his Palatines:

> "I can't explain why I dropped all other genealogical investigations to {commit myself to the Palatines}, but I did. It was as if nothing else mattered. The Palatines became my calling, and I felt it was my mission to tell their  story."

Hank has also felt urged to reach out to his genealogical colleagues, inviting them to share with him, and ultimately with you, the often highly intimate experiences we have had with those on the other side. The result is *Psychic Roots: Serendipity & Intuition in Genealogy.*  The voices may differ, but I hear many of the same beckoning messages that Hank hears. So I was delighted when he asked me to write this foreword.

What, then, is this book about? If I were allowed only one sentence, I would say this: *Psychic Roots* shows how **feeling** about one's ancestors, as well as **thinking** about them, usually results in a more successful search. Certainly, the research process is far more thrilling.

During a recent lecture, I announced to my audience, "I love Helen Law." This intimate statement was unplanned; it simply happened in an impromptu moment of passion. Some people might scoff and remark disparagingly that she has been dead for over 200 years; how could I possibly love her?  But it was - and is - an expression of true and valid feeling. Why should I not love this woman? During the past two years she has played a major part in  my life.

Helen Law has drawn me again and again to Aberdeen, Scotland, where she lived for some thirty years in the mid-eighteenth century. Each time I have wanted to learn more about her; during each visit, more of her has been revealed. She was an active woman about whom many records were created; so far, I have found her name recorded fifty-two times. Until recently, Scottish women kept their maiden or birth names, making it easier to reconstruct her life. For a few of her some three score years and ten I know what she was doing and where she was doing it, almost on a daily basis. Despite the fact that she could not write her name, court documents record some of her story in her own words. I know many of her tribulations, and can imagine the pain she must have felt; I also know of some wonderful moments in her life, and can share in the thrill she probably felt. Within the pages of *Psychic Roots* you will find the stories of dozens of genealogists, who have had similarly intimate experiences with ancestors long since departed.

A rational being knows that having passionate feelings for an ancestor is not enough. Many of the records about Helen Law have required me to think long and hard: I have drawn inferences from bits and pieces of knowledge about her; I have formulated these inferences into hypotheses susceptible to testing; and I have searched for evidence to test them. That thoughtful search has opened up records I would otherwise never have seen. By now, Judith Cripps, the City Archivist in Aberdeen, is well attuned to my keen interest in the lives of my ancestors and knows that I can usually report where they were living at any given date. Helen Law and her husband William Edward were living in Aberdeen in 1741, so she suggested that I search a record series naming hundreds of people who had purchased oatmeal from the town at a cut-rate price during a famine that year. The lists were made almost daily from January to June, so it seemed an impossible task to check every name; I set them aside. But then, I remembered a date that I could use to formulate a hypothesis. William Edward had been banished from the town as an outsider unable to earn a living. May 17, 1741, was the date on which he was to depart Aberdeen. Perhaps I could find his name among the oatmeal purchasers during the week prior to that date and then discover it missing thereafter.

The results were better than anticipated. William Edward made his last purchase on 16 May and Helen Law bought the family oatmeal from 18 May 1741 until the town supplies finally ran out. A subsequent search of the lists for the entire period told me how much the Edward-Law family had to eat that winter. If no other food were available, and other town records suggest there was none, then it is clear the family was starving.

Some of my fellow contributors talk of hunches and their intuition; I prefer the language of scientific method. But whether we test a formal hypothesis or follow up on an informal hunch; whether our thinking was conscious or, apparently, subconscious, the results of our mental processes have often produced wonderfully rich rewards. Nevertheless, some of my best finds have been serendipitous. I have found facts about Helen Law when actually I was looking for information about somebody or something else. Perhaps my most wonderful serendipitous experience was my discovery of her second husband, John Fraser, horsehyrer. This was a man about whom I had known nothing; their contract to marry was not recorded in the St. Nicholas (Aberdeen) parish marriage register.

It happened like this: I was looking in the back of Volume 6 of Aberdeen Warrants, hoping to find a list of people who - like William Edward - had been expelled from Aberdeen. Volume 5 had contained such a list, and I wanted to check for more. Volume 6 covers the period 27 December 1749 through 1757, and written on the inside of its back cover was an idiosyncratic record. It was an agreement by Helen Law, relict of John Fraser, horsehyrer, and her subtenants to vacate premises described as "the middle flatt outside the Justice Port," owned by John Smith, shoemaker. The discovery of this document is all the more remarkable because it was dated 10 November 1749. I might have missed it entirely except that Helen Law's mark was a beacon; I had seen her mark before and it was fixed in my memory. The pages of *Psychic Roots* are filled with many stories such as this.

Why do some of us genealogists have these and other seemingly nonrational experiences? When this book was gestating within Hank's heart and soul, he searched widely for answers. He did not have tunnel vision as many of us often do; he was receptive to all plausible explanations. These pages explore such topics as synchronicity (events that happen simultaneously with no apparent causal connection but with deep significance for those who experience them); numeracy (the mathematical probability of having a connection with any person you may happen to meet); intuition (a seeming sixth sense that a record will appear where it may or may not belong); genetic memory (the possibility that we inherit from our forebears some of the facts about our heritage). With the help of his colleagues, Hank explores each of them. You may not find a satisfying answer at the end of every explanatory avenue, but the very least you owe to yourself, to your ancestors, and to your descendants is to investigate each one.

Helen Hinchliff
Fulford Harbour, Canada
Easter 1993

# 1
# THE TRUNK

The first words I ever heard about genealogy were, "Hank, *don't* go in the trunk!" And my mother meant it!

In the lower basement of our home in San Leandro, California, was an old trunk whose contents and origins were unknown to me. I often had played in the basement on rainy days when I was home from school and had pretty well explored the nooks and crannies of that subterranean world - except for that one forbidden piece of history. It must have been nearly a hundred years old then and had faded to a dirty brown color, its brass latches and leather straps tarnished and worn from travel and years of disuse. What could be inside it, I wondered? That intriguing trunk was a puzzle that needed solving - at least to a slight, bookish, and somewhat introverted 8-year-old who probably had read one too many Hardy Boy Mysteries.

The ancient chest continued to entice me, almost beckoning to me to explore it. Finally one rainy and especially boring Saturday afternoon when my mom had gone shopping, I decided it was now or never. I raced down the basement stairs, heading toward the dark corner where the trunk lay. Trembling, I screwed in a bare electric bulb that dangled overhead. The faint light lent an eerie illumination to the scene below, which a cluster of silvery cobwebs made even more mysterious.

After struggling to clear away the cardboard cartons and all the household junk piled on top of my quarry, I was ready at long last to see what, for years, had been unseen. I cautiously approached the lid and eventually figured out how to open the double-locks, surprisingly still functional after all those years. To this day, I still can remember the apprehension and excitement I felt as I lifted the heavy lid and peered inside.

A strong, musty odor jarred me as I gazed at the yellowed contents on the top layer. It was the first time I had ever inhaled the pungent smell of very old books and papers, an aroma I would savor many times throughout my life as I searched in the open stacks of libraries and archives around the world. And - oh my! - what treasures my young eyes saw inside that old warhorse of a trunk. They far exceeded even what my wildest imagination had hoped for!

Ancient photos of every kind filled the huge container. Daguerrotypes with their shiny, magical mirror images - a pioneer woman lying stone-cold dead in her wooden coffin. Ambrotypes with their delicate glass negatives - bearded men in stove-pipe hats as sharply etched as the finest photographs of today. Tin-types showing beardless young lads hardly older than myself, all decked out in their civil war uniforms ready to fight the great fight and probably die an early death. And countless paper "carte de visites," the portrait calling-cards of the 1860s and 1870s, which undoubtedly had been left as small tokens of appreciation from guests who spent many a happy "at home" Sunday afternoon with my family long ago.

Then there were the fascinating documents and old bills from the 19th century. A copy of the 1890 will of my great-grandfather James Jones of Great Elm, Somersetshire, who once disowned his eldest son Henry after the boy had the audacity to tell him that he had no intention of staying "working class" forever in England and was leaving for a new life in America. A faded and rumpled bill for funeral services rendered "for the burial of one child" in 1863, a poignant reminder of the fragility of life during that tenuous time. And various old deeds to probably worthless property lying in the mined-out sections of the California Mother Lode Country.

Besides the family papers and photographs, the trunk was also a catch-all of other things preserved for God knows what reason. There were boxes upon boxes of ornamental hat-pins which numbered in the hundreds. Assorted feathers and collar-stays filled three manila packets. But balancing out those rather strange items, a collection of political campaign ribbons caught my eye immediately, especially the small banner that read "National Union Ticket of 1864, for President Abraham Lincoln, for Vice President Andrew Johnson" (with an added note that it was "sold for the benefit of sick and wounded soldiers"). A huge section of the storage space was taken up with brochures and large-sized picture albums from every exposition and world-class American Fair since the 1876 Centennial. My mouth fell open as I examined all the newspapers that my family had saved covering most major events since Lincoln's assassination in 1865. What a morbid thrill it was to read each successive edition of the *San Francisco Examiner* and see how the raging fire progressed throughout the city after the great earthquake in 1906.

And then there were the letters - literally hundreds of them. The envelopes themselves were interesting, some with advertisements for horse-drawn buggies, felt hats, razor strops, and other products distinctive of the times. The postmarks often were of towns and hamlets that no longer existed, relicts of a vanishing past enduring now only as dark black cancellations over faded two-cent stamps. But inside each envelope was the true gold. The letters within had been saved since 1863, and each and every one gave a reflection or a portrait of a family member I had never known. There were flowery notes on embossed stationary which were relics of my grandparents' courtship in the 1880s, models of etiquette which seemed to subtly belie a restrained Victorian passion. As I pored over the other correspondence, I began to really appreciate the beautiful qualities and true goodness of my grandmother Sarah Hillman Jones who had died long before I was born. I had heard that she was "one of a kind," an exceptional lady of great warmth and intellect. Her letters certainly exemplified those traits, especially the ones she wrote when she traveled from her San Francisco home to visit relatives back in upstate New York in 1882. This batch of correspondence was a revelation to me because my grandmother was vitally interested in her heritage and wrote down many wonderful anecdotes and lively sketches of earlier members of our family. She heard about the revolutionary war exploits of her ancestors from aged relatives who actually had known those patriots personally. The clipped, Yankee names of her own mother's family which she chronicled were almost laughable, so stereotypically "New England" were they in their sound. Abigail Dibble, Icabod Crippen, Dan Pomeroy, and all the others came alive, thanks to my grandmother's reporting, and they fascinated me. Of Icabod Crippen my grandmother wrote:

> "When {he} became of age {in 1783}, he received his horse, bridle, saddle, and a new suit of clothes called a 'freedom suit.' He tied up all of his belongings in a bandanna handkerchief and bought a teakettle, in the cover of which he cooked his bacon and fried his meat. When Icabod's children were married, they received their choice of a string of gold beads or ten sheep. His daughter Abigail, who married Noah Dibble in 1808, took the ten sheep and later regretted it since they were soon gone, while the other sisters still had their beads."

My grandmother's letters showed these Yankee ancestors to be not just merely names and dates, but the vital and real people who they really were!

The old trunk also contained many items relating to my grandmother's father Isaac Hillman. He was born in Shaftsbury, Vermont, in 1797, two years before the death of George Washington. I found this of great interest as my father was born in 1902, his mother in 1858, and then old Isaac, her father, in 1797: three generations in three centuries. It's sort of a Ripley's "Believe It Or Not," because my dad (who is still a vibrant and healthy 90 years old as I write this today) can say his *grandfather* was living when George Washington was alive!

I learned that Isaac Hillman was quite an eccentric character. He came from Troy, New York around "the Horn" to California during the gold rush. A life-long Methodist, Isaac opened a "Temperance House" in San Francisco where no liquor was ever served, quite a change from the wild and woolly Barbary Coast atmosphere of the city. He also peddled his "Hillman's Patent Medicines" on the busy streets of his new California home. Contemporary accounts in newspapers

My grandmother, Sarah Hillman Jones (1858–1921), surrounded by her children.
Did I inherit my "psychic roots" from her?

My great-grandfather, Isaac Hillman (1797–1879), my link to the
Irish Palatines.

of the day found in the trunk note that, as Isaac Hillman extolled the virtues of his restorative elixirs, he also would harangue his customers to repent of their sins and take the pledge to abstain from all spirits.

This somewhat holier-than-thou picture of my great-grandfather was pretty well shattered when I discovered the surviving recipe book for his medicines in a corner of the old chest. His "Cure-All" formula, which he advertised was "guaranteed to cure colds, dyptheria, bronchitis, larungitis, or any affection of the respiratory organs *(sic)*," starts off with requiring ten gallons of pure grain alcohol, cayenne pepper, and prodigious amounts of opium to brew it! Now I know why my father said the medicine knocked him out for days when he took it as a boy.

All the marvelous items found in that decrepit old trunk helped kindle a growing desire in me to find out more about my ancestors. I began questioning the elder members of my family about what they remembered of the family history. I was unrelenting in my persistence (and probably pretty obnoxious) as I pressed my uncles, aunts, and cousins for permission to dig in *their* attics and basements for more hidden treasures. In this way, other sources were gradually uncovered which, in turn, revealed new clues to explore.

I eventually discovered a tattered pedigree chart made by my grandmother in 1882 that took my father's family back years before the revolution and one line (the Fullers) eventually to the *Mayflower*. My mother's equally intriguing Danish lines were extended back to the 1600s via correspondence with relatives still in Europe. Frequent trips to the Sutro branch of the California State Library in San Francisco acquainted me with a wealth of genealogical literature just waiting to be examined. Sports and "normal boy stuff" held no interest for me: All I wanted to do was to climb the family tree.

I was becoming living proof of the old adage that says:

"Genealogy begins as an interest,
Becomes a hobby;
Continues as an avocation,
Takes over as an obsession,
And in its last stages,
Is an incurable disease."

I WAS HOOKED!

## 2
## *MY OWN JOURNEY*

But then, after exhaustively researching all the lines on both sides of my family, a very strange thing happened. I learned that my gold rush great-grandfather was not really named "Isaac Hillman" after all. He had been born "Isaac Bergmann" and was a descendant of a group of Germans who had originally settled in Ireland in 1709. This hearty band of emigrants, whose modern-day descendants were said to talk with a thicker brogue than Barry Fitzgerald but still went home each night to eat their sauerkraut, had a name that survived the centuries. They were called "Palatines."

Stumbling across this little, somewhat insignificant piece of information stopped me cold. I abruptly halted work on all my other ancestors and concentrated instead only on these specific Palatine German families. They fascinated me, and I wanted to know more ... much more! No comprehensive study had ever been made of the Irish-Germans' settlement. So, in 1960, while still an undergraduate at Stanford University, I began what eventually was to become a life-long task of chronicling this curious group. I can't explain why I dropped all other genealogical investigations to do this, but I did. It was as if nothing else mattered. The Palatines became my calling, and I felt it was my mission to tell their story.

This was all well and good, but I still had to make a living and function in the real world. In hindsight, I see now that my twenty years in the entertainment business as a singer and then an actor were a hidden blessing. When I began my career, my first job, after landing an RCA recording contract with my partner and life-long friend Dean Kay, was co-starring on the old ABC-TV "Tennessee Ernie Ford Show." The only network show out of San Francisco, it enabled me to finish my education at nearby Stanford without having to move to Hollywood. So many weekdays, after "blessing everybody's pea-pickin' heart" at the end of each show with "Old Ern," I would hightail it over to nearby Sutro Library, roll up my sleeves, and do some serious digging in the Palatine mines. I began to amass a treasure-trove of documented materials on these fascinating 18th-century emigrants.

The feast or famine aspects of "show-biz" continued to be helpful to my genealogical searches when I eventually journeyed south to Los Angeles to pursue an acting career. I found myself cubby-holed as a young character actor playing "best friend roles" in situation comedies. (Many of the "My Three Sons," "Love Boats," "Mork and Mindys," "Jeffersons," and "Patty Duke Shows" in which I appeared still come back to haunt me today via cable-TV). The movies also beckoned, and I continued playing innocents and inept bumblers in such Walt Disney films as "Blackbeard's Ghost," "Herbie Rides Again," "The Shaggy D.A.," and "The Cat From Outer Space" (eleven cats, all dyed to look the same, played the title role!). When I wasn't showing up for my 7 A.M. Disney call at the corner of Goofy Lane and Dopey Drive, I was working on other movie and TV lots - emoting as Ringo Starr's twin brother (after five grueling hours of make-up every day) in NBC's musical-comedy version of Mark Twain's "Prince and the Pauper," or being slaughtered by the Germans in Universal's "Young Warriors" and then giving equal time to the Japanese as they shot me down over Pearl Harbor in 20th Century Fox's "Tora-Tora-Tora!" It was fun acting with and learning from such talents as Peter Ustinov, Henry Fonda, Helen Hayes, Walter Brennan, Fred MacMurray, and Robin Williams. Some of my films turned out quite well. Others were real "dogs," such as the notorious "Village Of The Giants" which was once voted one of the 50 worst films of all time!

I never ever "got the girl" in any of these usually less-than-epic productions, but what I did get was time in between jobs to pursue my real love: genealogical research on the Palatines! Often I was months "between pictures" (what a great euphemism for unemployment!), and this hiatus allowed

Helping to pay for Palatine research: Peter Ustinov & Hank Jones in the Walt Disney production "Blackbeard's Ghost."

With Henry Fonda

With Tennessee Ernie Ford

With Robin Williams

me to continue combing libraries and archives for more data on this group which so intrigued me. In 1965, I finished my initial project and published a small book entitled *The Palatine Families Of Ireland* detailing the results of my research. But I couldn't let go: the Palatines had taken hold, still at the expense of all my other family lines. I realized that no similarly-comprehensive, thoroughly documented study had ever been made about the Palatines who went to *America* in the great exodus of 1709/10. Even though I had no known family connection with this other group, in 1969 I began a new Palatine project and plunged headlong into a study of these 847 German families who "took the risk" to emigrate and finally settled in colonial New York. This work all took place just prior to the time when personal computers were readily available as a helpful tool for research, so I did everything the old-fashioned way: longhand! I documented all my data with 17th- and 18th-century sources contemporary with the events. I extracted all Palatine baptisms, marriages, and burials from the churchbooks of their colonial communities and entered the information on family groupsheets, each sheet reflecting a Palatine couple and their offspring. By 1980 when I began writing my two-volume set *The Palatine Families of New York - 1710* incorporating this wealth of material, I had 17,000 family groupsheets, all handwritten, to work from.

A major thrust of my efforts was to find all the Palatines in their European ancestral homes and extend their lines as far back in time as possible. It was like a crusade to me, pinpointing and then tracing these Germans overseas. American records only noted a relative few of their precise villages of origin in Germany, but, undaunted, I persevered in my determination to discover their foreign roots. I bought a microfilm reader and purchased films of Palatine source materials from archives around the world. I immersed myself in their lives and times, sometimes feeling I was really more a resident of the 18th century than the 20th. Often I would digest the data on the films subconsciously, not really reading the information per se, but rather subliminally absorbing it all by staring at the screen for hours.

I gradually discovered the saving grace of my project was that these Germans rarely came to the new world literally alone: they emigrated in *groups* of friends and relatives from the same geographic regions in Europe and then stayed near and interacted with these same old acquaintances upon arrival. By studying and absorbing the records the Palatines left behind in their original, unalphabetized form, patterns of these emigrating groups leapt out at me. I then hypothesized just where certain families who were clustered together on these old documents might be found in Europe and instructed my chief German researcher, Carla Mittelstaedt-Kubaseck, to go literally village-to-village for me in the theorized regions of origin looking for these groups of emigrant families.

When Carla began her German searches for me in 1973, I had no real vested interest in any one particular New York Palatine family. To my knowledge, I descended from none of them. My goal was simply to find all 847 emigrant families overseas and tell their stories. No region or group was more important to me than any other, but, of course, we had to start somewhere. So I instructed Carla, just off the top of my head, to begin her initial investigations by looking for the 1709er Dieterich Schneider family and their "cluster" of emigrating neighbors who originated in the Westerwald area northeast of Koblenz. I can't really say why I found this Schneider so interesting, but he always had seemed to hold a strange fascination for me whenever I ran across his name in the old source materials.

Little did I know that this impromptu decision of where to begin the European leg of my project was to be my introduction to what some have called "The Twilight Zone of Genealogy," when unexplainable events and serendipitous experiences sometimes open doors and help us successfully find our ancestors. Even now, I still get a chill down my spine as I try to fathom what occurred.

What happened was this: our searches have gone on for twenty years now and over 600 of the 847 New York 1709er Palatine families have been successfully found in their ancestral homes via these intensive village-to-village investigations in Europe. And the *only* one I find that I am directly related to is the Dieterich Schneider family of the Westerwald - my first choice selected *totally at random* out of 847 names for Carla to seek in Germany!

I continued on. The more I immersed myself in the Palatines' world of the 17th and 18th centuries the more I began to feel a part of it. After years of increasing familiarity with each of the "1709er" families, they became "family" to me. I even developed strong likes and dislikes for particular Palatines. For example, I feel a warm affinity for emigrants from the Neuwied/Westerwald region of Germany, but a guarded suspicion of their compatriots who came from Württemberg in the 18th century. There's no rational explanation for this as these people died centuries ago, but it's there. And as my level of knowledge of these courageous people grew deeper and my feelings for them grew stronger, I felt secure enough with my subject matter to start taking some risks myself.

I had long been open to Carl Jung's ideas concerning the so-called "collective unconscious," a pool of knowledge ready to be tapped by intuition if only we learn to trust it. Jung believed that "we inherit the wisdom of the experience of our ancestors without ourselves having personal experience. All knowledge and wisdom are contained in our minds, and, when we discover 'something new,' we actually are only discovering something that existed in ourself all along." Inspired by these thoughts, I decided to test this intriguing concept: to see whether it might relate to some of my "seat-of-the-pants feelings" that occurred during my genealogical pursuits. Were these feelings valid? Could they really bring successful results in my searches if I "went" with them? This whole area intrigued me, and I was determined to explore it fully.

So I made a *conscious* decision to try to listen to my *sub*conscious, to trust my hunches if you will. I attempted to follow my intuition as well as my intellect in my searches. To my great delight, listening to my "inner voice" often reaped unexpected rewards. German documentation eventually verified many of my "educated guesses" as to emigrant origins. By allowing myself to be led in my searches, 600 "1709er" families and well over 1,000 later Palatine arrivals in the 1717-1776 period were found overseas in their ancestral European homes.

But even though I acknowledged the importance of the unconscious and the intuitive process, I still wondered what in heaven's name was going on? Why was I so preoccupied with a bunch of dead Germans who were long forgotten by most of my contemporaries? Why this sense of "mission" to study them at the exclusion of all other research, find their European origins, and then put them in family groups? Why did I feel sometimes as if another force was directing me in my searches? Why me!!??

I sought out books which might explain my obsession. I read widely in religion, metaphysics, parapsychology, past lives and reincarnation, the Edgar Cayce series of psychic readings, the "Life After Life" studies ... *anything* that would help me understand what was happening. I grew bolder in my studies, trying to absorb some of the more complex scientific research done on the subject of intuition and serendipitous events. I plowed through volumes which touched on Einstein's theory of relativity, quantum physics and the bending of time. I studied works such as Arthur Koestler's *The Roots of Coincidence* and pondered F. David Peat's *Synchronicity - The Bridge Between Matter and Mind.*

As my search continued, I wondered about the possibility of psychic roots. Family members often told me that my late grandmother, Sarah Hillman Jones, had a special gift. She would leave a room, and the others remaining would then pick an object or person therein to focus upon. When she returned, she could identify immediately the focus of everyone's concentration. According to those who had witnessed these remarkable happenings, my grandmother could do this with different people in various locations, and no code or signal was involved.

I also recalled certain nights during my very early childhood when it seemed as if I floated out of my bed, rose up into the sky, and then glided over the town looking down on the rooftops far below. I mention these weird journeys, indelibly-etched in my memory, because they were much more real than any dream I've ever dreamed, and had an intensity to them which I've never experienced again. They stopped when I was about five years old, but I'll never forget these youthful flights. Were they mere flights of fancy, or were they indeed the "out-of-body experiences" that one reads about?

And I remembered an event which made a deep impression upon me when I was about 12 years old. At a Boy Scout outing in Yosemite National Park, a fellow-camper named Dennis Ulrich had tripped, fallen into the river, and then was swept over a small waterfall, nearly killing himself on the rocks below. When we pulled him out of the water, cold and shivering, all he would talk about was how his entire life "flashed before his eyes." Dennis wasn't kidding: he was deadly serious in insisting that he had seen every event that had ever happened to him and every person he had ever known in those few seconds he was falling. He said that they all were as real as we were! I've never forgotten that.

Recalling all these events from the past, however disjointed, made me consider their validity and relevance to the present. And how my present world was indeed changing! The personal satisfaction I was receiving from my work in show business seemed to diminish the more I continued to investigate these phenomena and immerse myself in the Palatines' milieu. To my dismay, the world of genealogy was becoming much more attractive than the world of entertainment. Something had to give.

And it did. My mid-life career crisis all seemed to crystalize and come to a head in the mid-1980s when I returned from giving a lecture in Salt Lake City at a conference of the National Genealogical Society. I must admit my talk had been well received, and I walked in the door of my home feeling terrific, thinking that perhaps I had contributed something of value to the genealogical community. After unwinding from the trip, I went to check my telephone answering machine for any important messages that might have been left in my absence. The only message on the tape was from my commercials agent, who urgently inquired, "Can you be a dancing chicken at 3 o'clock?"

That did it. As much as I would have loved the nice residuals that my dancing chicken would have laid, I decided it was time to put away the grease paint (and feathers), move on, and concentrate fully on what had become my real love: genealogy! And so I did. Although continuing to do "voice-overs," I gave up all "on-camera" acting to devote myself to Palatine family research, and I've never ever regretted my decision.

From that moment on, some surprising and wonderful turns of events happened. My first books on the American immigrants, the two-volume *Palatine Families of New York - 1710,* all sold out, required a large second printing, and won the Jacobus Award as best genealogical work of the year. Then, I was elated to be elected one of the fifty Fellows of the American Society of Genealogists, an unexpected honor. My bookings for lectures and seminars (that I know helped fulfill whatever "hambone" traits still remained in me from my show-business days) increased, and I enjoyed welcome opportunities to share my love of genealogy with kindred spirits via these speaking engagements.

And then a real "left-fielder" occurred. On a dare, I took advantage of the Screen Actors Guild's decision to relax their prohibition against their members appearing as contestants on TV game shows and took the difficult examination to be on *Jeopardy!,* my long-time favorite quiz program. To my surprise, I passed the test and soon found myself facing Alex Trebek and some very tough competition on the show. I lasted three days on the program as "champion" and certainly enjoyed my winnings. But the real benefit from my *Jeopardy!* appearances was the chance to talk about genealogy and the Palatines on national television. The response from the viewing audience was astounding. For two months after the broadcasts, sacks of mail were delivered to my home from the Merv Griffin Production offices, all full of interesting questions about family history research and my Palatine project. The sales of my books even tripled! It all reached its zenith when a big batch of letters arrived one day with a tongue-in-cheek note from Trebek's secretary who griped, "Dear Hank, Alex is really ticked off. *You* received more mail this week than *he* did!"

Who would have thought this would happen? I sure didn't. I

attributed my good fortune to listening to my own "inner voice" which told me in no uncertain terms that it was time to cut the cord with show business and get on with making genealogy my life's work instead. But I still was intrigued with what was making me so obsessed with the Palatines. Were any of my genealogical colleagues having similar experiences, I wondered?

Or was it just me who seemed to be getting a bit too close to the butterfly net?

# 3
# THE SEARCH BEGINS

I had to find out. Somewhat timidly, I began to mention my interest in some of the psychic aspects of genealogy, first in conversations with my friends and then in my seminars. I even put a couple of paragraphs in my later books about how following my intuition as well as using my intellect in family research had sometimes brought successful results. Slowly, the responses to my comments began coming in. Audience-members started buttonholing me after my speaking engagements, eager to share research stories that had amused or puzzled them over the years. Several family historians sent me unsolicited recollections also detailing their out-of-the-ordinary and off-the-wall genealogical experiences. As this initial feedback grew, it gradually dawned on me: I was *not* alone! It was comforting to realize that my associates were having some extraordinary things happen to them also!

I decided to test the waters even further. I sent out 300 letters to noted genealogists around the world, inviting them to share their thoughts and any unusual personal experiences that they might have had along these lines. I especially wanted to hear about any serendipitous event or intuitive nudge they might have encountered while climbing the family tree. I always tried to make it clear to my colleagues that in no way was I trying to negate or minimize the proven and logical "scientific approach" to genealogy championed by the late Donald L. Jacobus and my fellow Fellows of the American Society of Genealogists. Their emphasis on thorough documentation and the careful weighing of evidence in constructing a family pedigree will always be inviolate in my view. But were other factors and forces - beyond the logical -

affecting our research? I wanted to know more. It was time to compare notes.

Over 200 individuals were kind enough to reply. The very first response I received from my big mailing was from Christine Rose of San Jose, California:

> "You've made my day brighter! I can relate well to your observations. Having immersed myself in Roses for thirty years, I can recall many times having 'off-the-wall' hunches that were later proven. And I've also experienced other phenomena that go beyond those hunches that I am totally unable to explain.
>
> Are we getting lots of help? I believe it 100%. For years, especially when I was teaching self-awareness seminars in the 1970's, I became fascinated with the whole realm of 'psychic' experiences. I read avidly of all aspects, from Edgar Cayce books, to out-of-body journeys, to reincarnation, and just about everything else. Various personal experiences have convinced me of the validity of some of these. What I am absolutely sure of is that there is much we do not understand, but that *does* happen!"

Whatever reservations I may have felt about venturing into this largely unexplored genealogical terrain were greatly diminished by Chris's letter and the similar replies that soon arrived. Prior to the mailing, I must confess to mentally preparing myself for the possibility of ridicule (or at least raised eyebrows) from some of my colleagues. The term "psychic" is defined rather matter-of-factly in *Webster's Dictionary* as simply "of the mind or psyche, beyond natural or known physical processes;" yet it can be a loaded word for many people, a real "red flag" to those who have a purely-logical view of the universe. But was I surprised! Only one less-than-enthusiastic response was received. It came from an editor of a prestigious journal who had published some of my Palatine material and book reviews. She was concerned that my new book might send mixed signals to less-experienced family historians and feared that the tabloids might sensationalize and distort my project with headlines such as "Astrology Genealogy Recommended by Internationally-Known Genealogist."

I also heard from one or two other friends who, I suppose, just were not on the same wave-length and were somewhat bewildered by my interest in this sort of phenomena. (One of my fellow genealogists, a super-bright and lovely woman for whom my admiration and respect knows no bounds, after receiving my mailing took me aside at a conference. She shook her head and, with a gentle smile, asked, "Hank ... have you ever received a letter that you just didn't know how to answer?")

Another colleague, one of our field's foremost authors and lecturers, did some soul searching and replied:

"Your invitation caused me to reflect and to search my memory for the kind of experience you will be including in your new book. But none of the discoveries I have made in the course of my years of genealogical activity (and historical and literary practice prior to my life as a genealogist) defy logical explanation. They were not mind-boggling or mystical discoveries, precisely because they resulted from methodological searching - from thinking rather than feeling - from the rational rather than emotional.

When I was unable to come up with one, I felt cheated, so I discussed the matter with a very dear and very close friend of mine. He is a truly spiritual man, a 'seeker,' who has known me well for many years. He said, given my temperament and attitude, I would not be able to recognize such an experience, and acknowledge it for what it was, even if I did have it, because I am too rigid and rational and structured. It would 'blow my mind' to admit it!"

But, by and large, my apprehensions were unwarranted. Most all of my responses suggested that I really had tuned into something! Distinguished Fellows of the American Society of Genealogists such as Francis James ("Jim") Dallett, Enid Adams, Walter Lee Sheppard, Jr., Jean Rumsey, and C. Frederick ("Fred") Kaufholz thought a book investigating this whole area would be welcome and wished me well. Brenda Dougall Merriman of Guelph, Canada, wrote:

"We have only met a few times, but your letter struck a most responsive chord in me, and I daresay you will get some avalanche of response. I say this because I think genealogists are incredible people, totally under-rated on a scale of consciousness measurement, if we had such a thing. When I read your letter, I said, 'Yes, Yes, I know what he means!"

Karen E. Livsey of Falconer, New York, said:
     "Your letter has been sitting on my desk 'haunting' me long enough. When I received it, I read it with many 'uh, huhs,' 'yeps,' and head-nodding."

Dale J. J. Leppard of Carlisle, Pennsylvania, noted:
     "You've really struck a chord with me on this project. I don't think I've ever met a dedicated genealogist, amateur or professional, who hasn't had some kind of similar story to tell."

But, understandably, sometimes my correspondents found it difficult to remember the stories! Marsha Hoffman Rising of Springfield, Missouri, commented:
     "What an interesting project! Your letter does strike a 'familiar chord,' but I can't pass along any real examples (of intuitive or serendipitous experiences) at present."

Melinde Lutz Sanborn of Derry, New Hampshire, observed:
     "I have been unerringly drawn to unexpected sources in several cases and can only marvel at the fortuitous nature of the inspiration. These include items like walking up to a gravestone in a cemetery and, even though the name is wrong, researching the person and making an unexpected link - or sitting next to someone in the Salt Lake City library who turns out to be working on the same lines ... My problem in responding to your letter is that I can't recall the details. I know it has happened to me, but the specifics that make a good story are lacking."

Winston De Ville of Ville Platte, Louisiana, said:
     "I've pondered the subject of your letter regarding intuition influencing genealogical research, and was sure I'd be able to recall such experiences during the last 30+ years

I've been at it. Such things have always intrigued me, and I do 'believe in' the concept you've put forth. But, alas, try as I might, I can come up with no specific incident."

Karen Mauer Green of Galveston, Texas, remarked:
"I certainly agree with you that intuition does play a part in our researching, and have often followed my hunch to find that it's true. Unfortunately, I don't have any experiences of the mind-boggling sort which would be useful."

And Marie Varrelman Melchiori of Vienna, Virginia, wrote:
"Oh, how I wish I had one of those wild or weird experiences to pass on to you. My own family research really needs some 'crystal ball' help. Unfortunately, the little bits and pieces that I have found have usually been right where they should have been."

But many other friends and colleagues could and did recall incidents  of the kind I was seeking. As their recollections poured in, I wondered if there might be some sort of commonality to the experiences? So I began arranging them all in categories, trying to see if any patterns of type or frequency might emerge out of the different occurrences. I also made careful record of my colleagues' views as to *why* they thought these phenomena might be happening. Their opinions were as intriguing as the experiences themselves. This project was getting to be fun!

As each letter was received, I typed the given experiences into my trusty personal computer (no 17,000 handwritten sheets for me anymore!). Whenever possible, I let each genealogist tell their own story in their own words, paraphrasing very little. Each and every incident reported in this book but one (and that one by request) has the name of a prominent family historian attached to it as its author. One of the great, old genealogical maxims is "Cite Your Sources," so I felt these personal references were absolutely essential to ensure credibility. As I read and studied the many experiences and comments, I soon began to realize that this was no longer *my* journey: it was *ours*! It was almost as if we were all traveling together on a common path.

So now, dear reader, it is time. Another basement trunk awaits. Join us in our search. Let us begin our mutual exploration into "The Twilight Zone of Genealogy." And what better place to begin a mysterious journey ...

... than in a cemetery!

# 4
# CEMETERIES: A GRAVE MATTER

To the truly dedicated genealogist, nothing can beat traipsing around an old cemetery looking for a dead ancestor's tombstone. These weatherbeaten old monuments are marvelous sources of vital statistics and personal information concerning our forefathers. No family historians worth their salt would let a few minor inconveniences (such as knee-high clumps of thistles, or swarms of attacking bugs) deter them from copying down a crucial date or making a good rubbing off the deteriorating surface of an old marker. In overgrown and abandoned graveyards, every amateur ancestral detective can blossom into a Sherlock Holmes, searching for clues that lead to solutions of long-standing family mysteries.

Cemeteries then are almost second homes to genealogists. As such, they often have been the settings for some wonderfully weird experiences related by my colleagues. As an example, one of my favorite cemetery stories was passed on by Mrs. Jean D. Worden of Zephyrhills, Florida. She was looking for the grave of her husband's ancestor Samuel M. Campbell, who had fought in the War of 1812. The Wordens didn't know where Campbell was buried, but on a hunch decided to check the stones of the Reservation Cemetery in Wyoming County, N.Y. which was just across the road from the family's property. As Mrs. Worden recalls,

"Usually when we go to a cemetery, we split up in sections to cover it all in a shorter time. My husband Gene had walked through his side, found nothing, and gone down the road to the car. I finally finished my side with no results also. But I had a feeling that Samuel had to be there, so I decided to double-check Gene's section.

As I walked through the foot high grass, I stumbled and fell flat on my face. Raising my head slowly, I looked up and realized that I had tripped over a marker which was only about six inches high. Gene saw me sprawled out on the ground and said, 'Are you o.k.?' I replied, 'Yes, but I wish your grandfather wouldn't grab me by the ankles like that!'

The war marker was in honor of the 27th Regiment of the New York State Militia in the War of 1812 - Samuel Campbell's own regiment."

Jane Fletcher Fiske of Boxford, Massachusetts, had a very mysterious experience relating to a cemetery. She writes:

"I grew up in the Hudson Valley, an only child of an only child, in a house that had been built by my maternal great-grandfather around 1845. All the relatives except my grandmother were dead before I was born, and she and my father both died before I was seven. This was a set-up to make a genealogist out of me for sure, because all the intriguing reminders, the hints, and the clues were there, but it was up to me to put the puzzle picture together. As I grew up, I began searching for the missing pieces.

One summer evening, somewhere around forty years ago when I was a college student, I was out driving around the countryside near home with my then boyfriend, looking for family gravestones. He was kind enough to keep me company on these jaunts, despite a lack of interest, and otherwise I wouldn't have had the courage to wander around some of the country burying grounds (which for some reason scared me silly at that age and gave me bad dreams at night). I was familiar with published records of Albany County gravestone inscriptions, but always hopeful that we might find something new.

We had covered the Indian Fields Burying Ground in the town of Coeymans, to which some of the graves of my Bull and Stuart ancestors had been removed when the Aquetuck Reservoir was built. I then had the bright idea of driving back to South Bethlehem where there was an old farmhouse I'd passed countless times throughout my childhood. I told my friend, 'Mother says that house belonged to the Soop family once.' (Soop was my middle name, and my Soop ancestors settled in Bethlehem, Albany

County before the revolution. Our house was still thought of by old-timers in town as the 'Soop place,' despite the fact that marriages had over the years carried it into the Bull and Fletcher families.)

My friend was agreeable, so we drove the ten or fifteen miles back to South Bethlehem. I went up to the front door of the house which was set back from the road among the trees. A woman answered my knock, and I asked her if by any chance there was a Soop burying ground on the property. She admitted there was, and rather reluctantly led me around to the backyard where a handful of broken stones lay in a pasture open to cows and chickens. There on the ground were the gravestones of my great-great-great grandfather Conrad Soop, a Revolutionary soldier, and his wife Elizabeth Becker, along with those of a granddaughter and her children. It was still light enough to take photographs, for which we stood the stones up as best we could. Afterwards, we went into the house where Mrs. Cass, the recently-widowed owner, showed me the original leases to Conrad Soop from the patroon Stephen Van Rensselaer. They had been left in the house, which had evidently gone from Conrad to his youngest son Frederick and then to Frederick's daughter.

There would be nothing particularly unusual about this experience, except that when we got home and I told my mother where we had been, she looked at me and announced, 'I never knew that any Soops lived on that property.' Later, as I discovered more details from land records, and found that the son Frederick Soop was buried in the same cemetery as our own Soops - in a different lot and without a stone marker - she was as surprised as I was to learn about these relatives who had once lived so close but had been totally forgotten.

Where did the impulse come from that summer evening to send me up to the door of an old farmhouse? It was more than intuition; it was a specific idea that I thought my mother had told me something that I later realized she could not have. Maybe it was my own unconscious 'memory' in the Jungian sense. I tend to believe it was one of those times when some consciousness in another dimension is able to reach through the barriers of time and space to give us a helpful or playful nudge."

One of the most common occurrences centering around cemeteries is the speedy and uncannily direct way in which some descendants have discovered their ancestors' tombstones. Nick Vine Hall of Australia notes:

"I have had people on my radio shows tell me they have walked into large cemeteries and gone straight to the graves of their ancestors, even though they had never visited the cemeteries previously."

His friend Professor Mark L. Wahlqvist of Melbourne endorses Nick's statement. He was trying to locate the graves of his Aunt Selma and her husband Arthur David Smith on his first visit to the large Woodbridge Eastside Cemetery in New Haven, Connecticut. The local fire chief left him at the gate of the cemetery. As Professor Wahlqvist then recalls:

"I anxiously and excitedly drove down the main road towards the rear of the cemetery, not knowing where to begin my search for Arthur David Smith's grave or whether I could reasonably expect that Aunt Selma might be buried there as well. As I turned the vehicle left at the end of the road, I looked out the window and the first grave I saw was that of Arthur David Smith. I then lifted my eyes directly behind, by three or four metres, and there was the headstone of Selma Sofia Wahlqvist (1874 - 1959). Tears welled up in my eyes, and I fell to my knees with both joy and sadness; joy that I had found her, and sadness to know that, after leaving Sweden, my grandfather and this woman, his youngest sister, had never met again."

Oran S. Emrich of Kansas City, Missouri, recounts a similar tale:

"Several years ago, I went to Butler County, Pennsylvania, to research the Michael Emrich family, early pioneers in the county. In the library there, I found that Michael was buried in the West Branch Cemetery which was located about six miles south of Butler. After driving to the location, I parked outside of the cemetery and proceeded to walk down the middle of the rows of graves, not looking to either side, wondering where to start. About three fourths of the way through the cemetery, I

looked up and there as big as life was the marker for
'Michael Emrich, died 31 January 1856, aged 68 years, 7
months, and 28 days.' It was as if I had been drawn to the
stone by a magnet!"

William W. Berkman of Colorado Springs, Colorado, has
his version of this same basic story:

"I learned that my relative William M. Berkman had
buried several of his children in a Northfield, Minnesota
cemetery. On our way to Wisconsin for an annual reunion
with friends from kindergarten days, we stopped by this
cemetery and drove in to look for the gravestone to see if it
could provide any clues for research. Not knowing the
cemetery, we stopped the car and got out to look around.
Unbelievably, I had stopped within a few feet of the
gravestone, which looked like it had been engraved the
day before. It was an experience that sent chills up my
spine!"

After I had given a seminar to her group, an officer in the
Palatines To America organization came up and told me of an
even stranger experience along these lines. She had known for
years where her grandfather's grave was, but had never
learned where her grandmother was buried. She was
determined to find her tombstone and decided to make a trip to
the home county where they both lived. On what she describes
as "a total lark," she went to a town in that county where her
grandparents had never resided. She went on to explain,

"I just felt I should go there, I don't know why.
Encountering a resident of the town, I asked directions to
the local Catholic cemetery. In hindsight, this was a
strange thing for me to do, as my grandparents were
Protestants and not Catholics at all. Continuing to follow
my intuition, I then drove directly to this cemetery, got out
of the car, and walked straight to my grandmother's
grave!"

Carol Willsey Bell of Youngstown, Ohio, and her friend
Helen L. Harriss of Pittsburgh had a tandem eye-opener in a
cemetery in Canonsburg, Pennsylvania:

"We had gone there hopefully to find a certain gravestone of a member of the White family who had lived in the area. But the cemetery was much larger than we expected, and we really didn't have a clue as to where to look. As the cemetery office was not opened, we decided it would be a useless hunt, and that it would be wiser to return another day. So we pulled the car off the road into a spot where we could back out to turn, and there, right in front of the car, was the very stone we had hoped to find, surrounded by many other stones of the White family. How often could that happen?"

**Judge John D. Austin of Queensbury, New York, remembers,**

"My genealogical friend Gordon Remington of Salt Lake City helped show me the sights there in the fall of 1986. Knowing that I was from Queensbury, Warren County, New York, he asked me, just before I left, if I had any record of the tombstone of Thomas Johnston, who died in 1866, a transplant to Queensbury from Scotland. I flew home and rather promptly checked my records for the Scotch Cemetery out Bay Road. But, strangely, I found nothing.

The next weekend I was tending the graves of my deceased sons at Sunnyside Cemetery, about a half-mile from home. Before leaving, I rambled the grounds a bit, as is my wont, and discovered a stone for Thomas Johnston at the end of the very row in which my sons are buried! As an added delight that all genealogists can appreciate, the accompanying marker for Thomas Johnston's wife Catharine Glencorse, who died in 1842, specifies her birthplace as Lochmaben, Dumfriesshire."

**Dale J. J. Leppard of Carlisle, Pennsylvania, had another memorable experience in a cemetery.**

"The first genealogical field trip I went on as a young boy was an historical tour of the Tulpehocken (a lovely area of Pennsylvania largely settled by Palatines). The only thing I can remember about that trip was the Reed homestead which, as it turns out, was the farm of my 5th great grandfather Johann Peter Rieth and his father Johann Leonhardt Rieth. At that time, I had no reason to even imagine I was related to that family, yet the memory of the homestead being pointed out is so clear to me that it almost seems like I knew that it would someday be important to me.

I believe it was in the Spring of 1986 that I first learned of my line of descent from the Reed/Rieth family of Tulpehocken. Soon after, I discovered that my ancestor Johann Leonhardt Rieth (1691-1747) was buried in the Reed's Church cemetery at Stouchsburg in Berks County. The prospect of finding the grave of an ancestor who died almost 240 years earlier intrigued me, and I was determined to visit the site. I drove about 50 miles to Stouchsburg, and without a map or directions was quickly able to locate the Reed's cemetery. It was a warm, clear, and calm afternoon. I parked my car near the gate and grabbed my camera. I walked into the cemetery and continued walking without being aware of where I was going. (It must be understood that I had never been to this place before, nor had I yet found any of the many existing photographs and articles about Johann Leonhardt Rieth's tombstone.)

Suddenly, as I was walking, I felt a shiver run down my spine, and I stopped and turned. There, behind me, stood an old tombstone emblazoned with a skull and crossbones! I drew closer and, as I struggled with the crudely spelled German inscription, I read 'Here lies Johann Leonhardt Rieth....!'

I'm still not sure whether I 'found' him or he 'found' me! Since then, I have gone back several times, but I will never forget that first encounter with my ancestor's grave."

Ken D. Johnson of Grand Island, Nebraska, had quite an experience on his last visit to New York's lovely Mohawk Valley:

"Do the dead reach out from beyond the veil to request the aid of the living? This question has been bothering me of late. In more than one instance while researching, I have felt an indescribable need to look at something again. Books, microfilm, and gravestones have beckoned me to return.

I was bent on documenting the life-span of Captain Jost House of Minden Township in Montgomery County. His gravestone data appear in various transcripts, but all differ

The tombstone of Jost Haus (Joseph House).

in their given dates. I have traveled to this graveyard six times in the last three years with various historians and was shocked to see the general decay of all the gravestones. On each of these trips, I photographed Jost's headstone.

The day I was to leave New York, I made my final trip to the Geisenburg Graveyard. As I stood by the grave bemoaning the decay of the stone and wondering how the correct date could ever be retrieved, the cloudy sky parted, and beams of light reached down and touched the stone. Suddenly the writing appeared clear and bold. The phenomenon only lasted about three minutes. I photographed the headstone twice. I cannot explain why, but I have been told by friends who have since rechecked the stone at the same time of day that its dates continue to be unreadable."

Ken goes on to ponder:

"Was this a case of the dead helping us? Was it a freak of nature? Was it sheer coincidence? I shall never know. As a member of the L.D.S. church, I am happy in my belief that Jost House himself reached out to me, desiring the rituals of our faith. But regardless - the story is entirely true!"

The "Relatively Speaking" column in *The Genealogical Helper* often contains marvelous incidents of a serendipitous nature contributed by readers. The Everton Publishers gave me permission to relate the following story, sent in by Carol Montrose of Reynoldsburg, Ohio, in 1989:

"Late last summer, I called my distant cousin Jim Bell and asked if he knew where my Aunt Kate (Katherine Rettic Stegmeier) was buried. If I got the death date from the gravestone, I would then have a date to check her death record at the courthouse. Hopefully the death record would list Kate's parents or her birthplace, at least some clue.

Jim was vague about the location of the cemetery where his grandmother was buried. Just 'over near Glenmore, Ohio' several miles from the Rummel's burial place but not too far out of my way. You guessed it! Three small and one large cemeteries later, no luck. It was getting late on this beautiful afternoon, and I still had a hundred miles to drive home. I finally gave up, temporarily of course, and reluctantly headed my car toward home. My son Geno was sleeping on the front seat, the late summer fields had lost his interest hours before.

Just a few miles south, I spotted a very colorful hot air balloon in the sky, heading toward us. Quickly, I wakened Geno to look at the balloon. It seemed to be dropping as it moved toward us. It was going to land and not too far from where we were. How exciting! On the spur of the moment, we both decided to go see the balloon land. The car just seemed to turn the same way as the balloon, and we chased it for about a mile. The balloon seemed to dip into a field just ahead of us as if to land. At the corner of the field, the Schumm Church stood with its cemetery across the road.

I parked in the church parking lot and, as Geno headed toward the field behind the church to see the balloon, I headed to the cemetery. I certainly couldn't pass up the opportunity to check this one out, even though I had no idea that I had any relatives buried there. It was in the area of several families I had been working on. Nearly the first stone I looked at had the name 'Frederick Stegmeier!' The family I had searched for all afternoon. Right there in the front row!

Eagerly I searched. Yes, there was Katherine's grave, her husband, and two more of her children. I copied the information and quickly crossed the road to join Geno and the balloon. The balloon hadn't landed, but had gained altitude, skipped over the trees, and continued on its flight. Geno was disappointed because it had not landed, but excited that he had seen a hot air balloon up so close. Of course, I was ecstatic to not only find 'Aunt Kate,' but some of her children too.

My question to you is: Why did the balloon drop just at the time we crossed its path? Why did we decide to chase it? Why did it choose that particular place to dip as though it was going to land? Who helped me find Aunt Kate? Or did she find me??!!"

Although slightly in a different vein, my all-time-favorite cemetery story was contributed by my good friend William C. Kiessel of Bearsville, New York:

"Early in life I was fascinated with history. As an interested teenager in the 1930's, I asked questions and preserved family history dates and anecdotes as related to me by both my father's elderly mother and also from my mother's genteel father. These wonderfully loquacious octo- and septuagenarian grandparents were able to take me back to their own grandparents with names and dates to the late 1700's; a definite springboard to begin my later extensive ancestral research.

On my three grandparent family lines everything was informatively detailed. However, when I came to my mother's mother's O'Brien-Vervenne families, I drew an absolute impassive blank. It was a taboo subject of child abandonment and not discussed by my grandmother. Well, perhaps not an absolute complete blank, as I had one vague, very vague clue. My mother, dredging back into her memory, remembered as just a toddler walking hand in hand with her mother and in passing by an old church cemetery her mother saying, 'Papa is buried in there.' Not very much to go on.

But what old cemetery and adjacent to what old church were they walking past? There were really only four very old churches with adjacent cemeteries to fit that limited description. There was 'Old South' in Bergenfield, 'Old North' in Dumont, 'Old Hook' in Westwood, and possibly the cemetery near the Dutch Reformed Church in nearby Paramus, all encompassing what had been, roughly, the Schraalenburgh area of New Jersey.

In 1937, the 10th of July to be exact, on a beautiful Saturday afternoon, directly after lunch I took Dad's car - we lived in Tenafly - and drove over to nearby Bergenfield to begin my Vervenne research. I located the pastor's home next to the 'Old South' Church, but the pastor did not have the old records. He gave me directions to the cemetery custodian who lived on the other side of town. With the verbal directions etched in my mind ('go right, go left, turn here, turn there, then right, then left, the corner gas station, etc., etc., and then to the second house up the block on the left hand side'), I finally reached my destination of Cleveland Street. Unbelievably, I had negotiated all the endlessly confusing twists and turns. But by the time, ultimately, I located Cleveland Street, I understandably had forgotten whether it was the second house on the left or on the right hand side.

Most of the mistakes in life I have made - and there have been many - I have regretted. However, the mistake I made at about two o'clock on that beautiful Saturday afternoon on the 10th of July, 1937 was the best, most enduring, and consequential of my entire life! I counted up the second house and then - eternally grateful - I mistakenly went to the house on the right. Hopefully I knocked on the door, cheerfully optimistic of finding out about Abram Vervenne, my mother's long-deceased grandfather. That door I knocked on should be preserved in bronze because it was opened by the liveliest, cutest, prettiest girl I had - and have - ever seen. And now, 55 years later, I am still totally mesmerized by the still personable vision of exciting loveliness - the former Miriam Anne Dodd and now Mrs. William C. Kiessel. As we talked, Cupid so impaled me that I completely forgot I had intended to go across the street and look for possible cemetery records. I never did and instead happily floated all the way back home to Tenafly.

For two years Miriam and I "dated" as it was then called in those platonic days (daze?). We worked in different insurance companies in New York City until I entered Asbury College in Kentucky in 1939. Shortly after Pearl Harbor in 1941, I joined the famed 36th Division and served in Africa, Italy, France, Germany, and Austria. I returned home to New Jersey in 1945 after an almost total absence of six years. On my return, Miriam Anne and I rekindled our affection while I completed my education, this time remaining in New Jersey at Rutgers College and then on to graduate studies at New York University. While on the staff of the New York State Education Department, Miriam Anne and I were married on Saturday the 3rd of December 1949.

Many genealogists would be disappointed that I was so unsuccessful in locating when and where my grandmother's father, Abram Vervenne, died and was buried. I totally disagree!

Unequivocally, I believe my failed cemetery research trip 55 years ago on that beautiful Saturday afternoon on the 10th of July 1937 was absolutely without question the most successful failure in my entire genealogical career."

**I LIKE THAT!**

Bill & Miriam Kiessel today.

# 5
# THE RIGHT BOOKS
# & THE WRONG MICROFILMS

It's a given that cemeteries can be somewhat spooky. But what about other things genealogists have to deal with? Books and microfilms, for instance. Can a book or a film have a life of its own? Maybe so, at least according to some of the letters I've received.

One of the most common experiences that my colleagues have shared regarding books is the volume, usually encountered by chance, that falls open to a crucial page which then happily is found to contain long-sought-for family information. Helen L. Harriss has a textbook example of this phenomenon. She writes,

"Probably the first unusual episode that I experienced was early in my research. I had gone to the library to do research on my mother's family. I pushed a pile of books aside on a table in order to work, and the top one fell off. The strange thing was that it opened to a page with an account of my father's family, complete with charts, etc. At this initial stage of my investigations, I wouldn't have known to look in that particular book - a bound volume of the *New England Historical & Genealogical Society* Magazines. Naturally, that day, I worked on my father's Gilberts!"

Elissa Scalise Powell of Wexford, Pennsylvania, expands on this in an article entitled "Original Thoughts on Serendipity:"

"Serendipity is a part of genealogy, and it happens when you least expect it. For instance, (it occurs) when you are very busily copying baptismal data on your family out of a book in a library, and something calls to you to get up and take the books you are done with to the return cart. On top of the return cart is a cemetery book that you 'happen' to pick up and leaf through ... and lo, and behold, there is your spouse's family, all buried in one small family plot, with names, dates, and directions to the cemetery."

It seems that sometimes a serendipitous event involving books can be of the gentlest sort, nothing earthshaking but quite helpful. Karen E. Livsey is a genealogist, author and librarian who feels unnerved when:

"I often open a card catalog drawer and stick my finger into the cards at exactly the place for which I am looking! Or when I turn exactly to the right page in the book after looking up a subject in its index."

Karen goes on to ponder other incidents:

"Why did my step-mother pick up two old looking books at my grandfather's when they removed some furniture from the house? She thought they might be interesting to look at later. One book turned out to be my great great grandfather's order book for tombstones during the 1850's and 60's. The other was his wife's scrapbook kept from before their marriage. My Aunt then proceeded to clean out the house, later burning much of 'all that old stuff no one would ever buy at an auction."

Mary McCampbell Bell of Arlington, Virginia, one of the vibrant forces in modern genealogy, had a helping hand from one of her own books:

"I was discussing my Dad's memoirs with his sister Ruth. Daddy had talked about going out west during the time he was in college with his uncle and aunt, John Stoffel and his wife Edith (Newman). Casually he mentioned having seen some cousins named Mountcastle on the trip. I asked Aunt Ruth who these people could be, as I had never heard of them, and she said that they must be related to the Newmans. I had compiled a 75 page genealogy of my dad's maternal Rankin family and remembered that there were some Newmans mentioned in the manuscript. When I pulled it out and opened it, my finger was lying not only on the correct page, but right on the sentence where it told that one of the Newman girls had married a Mr.

Mountcastle! I could have spent hours searching through that thing looking for the Newmans. Maybe it's just a quirk of chance, but I'd like those chances to come more often!"

Following a simple hunch while perusing books in a genealogical library often brings unexpectedly successful results. Lahoma Lindeman of Layton, Utah, recalls:

"I have done quite a bit of genealogical work in the Family History Library in Salt Lake City. On numerous occasions I have been doing research, and, on an impulse, I would take a book from the shelves and open it up to find information on the families I was working on."

Carol Willsey Bell remembers when a brand-new researcher came into the library with a batch of Columbiana County ancestors.

"He told me he had gathered family stories, including one in which two children in a family were 'given up' when their mother died. One was a girl named Ida Davis who was adopted by a family who had lost a daughter named Ida. He wondered if there was any chance of finding out more about it. I told him the standard line that adoptions are hard to come by, but that sometimes they are 'buried' in other records.

When I came home that night, I had to deal with replacing the ink cartridge in my printer since it had given up two nights before. I decided to run a test copy to see how it was doing, grabbed a disk that was sitting on the desk, looked at the list of files, and chose 'Adoptions,' telling it to run page one. Imagine my surprise when on that page was the complete record relating to the same Ida Davis! Fate had led me to print a page from that file."

Dr. W. Cary Anderson of Decatur, Arkansas, remembers an event that took place in the Memphis Library in the late 1960s:

"I was there to work on my Fountain/de la Fontaine family. As I was leaving the library, I passed the Kentucky Section unknowingly. I happened to look up and saw a book entitled '*Marriages of Nelson County, Kentucky*.' I knew of a James White, born about 1804 in Kentucky according to the

1850 Census of Knox County, Indiana, and his wife Louisa. I pulled the book down, checked the index, and found the marriage of 'James White to Louisa Thomas, daughter of William F. Thomas.' I wasn't even working on White nor had any thought of doing so when that happened. It was as if I was being pushed to that book. This eventually enabled me to trace William F. Thomas back to Thomas Thomas who arrived in Maryland in 1635, a connection I never would have made without that not so gentle shove."

Cary adds,

"Hank, it actually gives me a strange sensation now as I write this - rather scary."

Dorothy M. Lower of Fort Wayne, Indiana, has another story of an intuitive nature relating to a book:

"The truly fascinating subject of intuition often plays an important part in genealogical research. According to family tradition, my great grandmother, Mary Johns, came to America from France with her parents in the 1830's, when she was four years old. Her father died on the voyage and was buried at sea. Mary and her widowed mother settled in Fort Wayne. When Mary was twelve, she was orphaned by the death of her mother, and she lived and worked for two prominent Fort Wayne families.

Having only this background, I worked for several years checking passenger lists, naturalizations, guardianships, church records, and records of local French families. One day I came across a slim little book of Bible records compiled by our local D.A.R. chapter. The book appeared to be well-indexed, but there was no listing for the name "Johns." However, *something* prompted me to check the book page by page. The first records were of a local Harrison family. Sure enough there was information on a daughter, Matilda, who married a Morgan Johns. She died the year that Mary would have been twelve. Further research revealed that Mary was born at Muncie, Indiana where her father was a contractor who died broke in the poorhouse. Incidentally, the two families with whom Mary had lived were those of Matilda's sisters. So much for tradition!"

Myrtle Stevens Hyde of Ogden, Utah, borrowed a copy of Jacobus' *Families of Old Fairfield* from the New England Historic Genealogical Society in Boston. She remarks,

"I normally don't approve of people writing in books, but in that volume someone had written in the margin by 'unplaced' Ephraim Adams (an ancestor we were seeking): 'D.F.P.A. Lineage #4249.' These letters meant nothing to me then, but I later found out that they were initials for 'Daughters of Founders and Patriots of America.' This society kindly furnished information about Member #4249, and I corresponded with her aged widower in Michigan. Soon afterward, a cousin attended school in that state, visited the man, and found wonderful records!"

At times, it appears that a genealogical book almost chases us down so that we'll use it. Christine Rose tells of an incident that happened to a now-deceased member of her nationwide Rose Family Association. The woman had been searching for her Phineas Rose in the library, going through all the shelves, when a book fell from a shelf right onto her head. She picked it up, idly leafed through it, and then made the startling discovery that it contained the wonderful revolutionary records of her ancestor. She had not known previously that he had even served in the war, and said she wouldn't have ever thought to look for a record of such service. She said her ancestor wanted to "hit her over the head" so that she would know, in no uncertain terms, of his pride at having revolutionary service in the war that created our nation.

Doris D. Rooney of Dodge City, Kansas, had another experience along these lines.

"How much do eleven large 3-ring notebooks of genealogical charts and data weigh? Admittedly too much for one 17-foot-long shelf to hold! One day, I watched the shelf start to sag and buckle. Then all the books on the shelf succumbed to the domino effect, tumbling down to the desk top below and then on to the floor. The *first* book I picked up opened to a page of queries published back in the 1930's in the genealogical column of a Mohawk Valley newspaper. One item on that page had the name of a family I had been seeking for many years. Still more unbelievable, is that when I wrote to the person who had inserted that query forty years before, I received an answer with the information I needed to document the family in my records."

An old Family Bible finally found Mary Ann Cole of Kenosha, Wisconsin:

"I had spent the past several years trying to track down my 'missing' grandfather, Carmine E. Shinn who had been a Western Union operator in Kansas City, Missouri 1889-1892. It took me a long time to track him back to his birth family in Putnam Co., Indiana. I was then able to trace his parents and sibling to Indianapolis by using a combination of census records, city directories, and WPA Indexes - but, alas, NO Carmine!

While I was so diligently searching death and cemetery records from Chicago to Kansas City, about four years ago a young man walking down an alley in Indianapolis found an old Bible laying in the dirt. He picked it up and took it home to show to his mother. His mother, not knowing what to do with it, gave it to her sister, Pamela Garrity of Camby, Indiana. Pam realized that the Bible - with its handwritten accounts of births, deaths and marriages, newspaper clippings, obits, photographs and poems - would be very valuable to family members.

Pam then started her own search to reunite the Bible with the family. She called all the Shinn listings in the Indianapolis phone book (who all claimed they had never heard of the people listed in the Bible). Pam even visited the cemeteries where some of the family were buried and examined the records to see if she could find a married name of a daughter in the family. Meanwhile, the Bible stayed on the shelf in her closet while everyone told her she would never find that family!

In July of 1990, I placed a query in the *Indianapolis Star* asking for information on my Shinn family. On 25 July 1990, I then received a wonderful letter from Pam telling me of the Bible, and how she had been searching for the family. Not wishing to trust the Bible to the U.S. Mail (and push my luck at having it lost again) - I drove down to Camby,

Indiana, met Pam and her family, and brought the Bible home. The information in the Bible answered all our questions about my grandfather Carmine. It even recounted his career in New York City and Cincinnati with the Board of Trade (no wonder I hadn't been able to find him).

In all, it seems as if a whole series of small miracles happened in order to reunite the Bible and our family! It is still quite a mystery to all of us just how the Bible came to be laying in an Indianapolis alley 70 years after the last entry was made in its pages. We are very thankful that Pam and her nephew both went to the time and trouble to save the Bible and look for our family!"

**Mary Keysor Meyer of Mt. Airy, Maryland, tells a fascinating tale that happened to her:**
"Once upon a time, many years ago in the 1950's, as a resident of Cazenovia, New York, I was advertising myself as a professional genealogist, at the huge sum of $2.00 per hour plus gas money (then about 35 cents per gal.). One day I received a request from one Dwight Brown, a resident of Riverside, California, asking me if I would consider doing some research on his Brown and Smith families of Madison County, New York on which he had been researching for 30 years. Well what does one say in response to such a request? You just sit down and become hysterical, which I did.

After I calmed down and got myself in hand, I wrote the poor demented soul and said, well of course, naturally, if he wished me to do some research on his Smiths and Browns (ha! ha! ha!) I would be happy to oblige, but ... I could not promise him that I would find one iota of information. He replied, sending a check for the munificent sum of $15.00 and told me to do what I could.

After giving it much thought, and studying the records of the local church which Nathan Smith, Mr. Brown's ancestor, had built, I reasoned that inasmuch as one Jonathan Smith, another member of the same church who had arrived in the area some years prior to Nathan, had come from Stockbridge, Massachusetts ... perhaps Nathan might also have come from that town.

So off I traipsed to the Syracuse Public Library, which has one of the finest collections of local history and genealogy in New York State, expecting to find nothing at all, but still holding out that one hope. I went to the stacks - open stacks, that is - and found the published *Vital Records of Stockbridge, Massachusetts*, pulled the book from the shelf and proceeded to examine it.

Much to my astonishment, here was Nathan Smith, the record of his marriage to Anna Damon; the baptism of his children, Nathan's own baptism, the name of his father and his grandfather, and even the name of the town in which his grandfather had formerly lived. There was even the record of the marriage of one of Nathan's sons in which it was stated that he was from Cazenovia, New York - my home then.

How, I wondered, had my client - in 30 years of research - missed this information - in the most obvious place? I was greatly excited and painstakenly copied all the information. (This was in the days before the Xerox machine was invented.) When I had finished this laborious task, I turned to the title page of the book in order to record my source of reference.

My God! I gasped! I did not have the *Vital Records of Stockbridge, Massachusetts*. I had the *Vital Records of Sturbridge, Massachusetts*. Did the Great God of Genealogy guide my hand that day ... or was it pure, stupid, dumb luck?

Whatever ... to Mr. Brown, my client, I became the greatest!"

**Judge John D. Austin of Queensbury, New York, can identify with Mary:**

"In 1965, I attended a research conference at the NEHG Society in Boston. A fellow conferee from Marion, Indiana, sought to learn more about Asa Rice of 'W. Creek.' He had concluded the 'W. Creek' referred to White Creek, Washington County, New York. We were standing in the stacks, and I pointed out Gertrude Barber's *Abstracts of Washington County Wills*, a typescript bound in red. I thought I handed him the correct volume, but inadvertently I pulled out a nearby book, identically bound, containing her *Abstracts of Warren County Wills*.

'Here it is!' he exclaimed. An abstract of the will of Asa Rice was found therein, the testator having moved in old age from White Creek, Washington County, to Luzerne,

> Warren County. This error was among the contributors to an
> interesting article 'A Tradition in Search of Its Origin,' by
> Stanley Perin in NEHGR 121: 29 - 36."

Besides having access to countless books to help facilitate
research, today's genealogists also are blessed in having
thousands of crucial old records available on microfilm and
microfiche to help in their investigations. So it should come
as no surprise, then, that the microfilm reader has been the
setting for many an unusual event experienced by family
historians while tracing their ancestors.

One such occurrence was related to me at a genealogical
conference in Andover, Massachusetts, in 1991 by Alice W.
Long of Mt. Desert, Maine. A few years ago, while on a five-
day research trip to the Provincial Archives of Nova Scotia in
Halifax, Alice made a new friend in Lois Wade Thurston of
Gardiner, Maine. As they became acquainted and spent time
together, they compared genealogical war stories and talked of
their common interests. Lois eventually told Alice about her
ancestry, including the lines that continued to stump her even
after years of searching for them. Several weeks after this
conversation, Alice was working in the film section of a
genealogical library and was delivered a different roll of
microfilm than the one she had ordered at the front desk. As it
was the completely wrong locale, Alice had no use for it. But
something made her skim the film's contents anyway, and
there on that "wrong" roll of film was the very family that
her new friend Lois had recently told her about - the one she
had been unsuccessfully looking for for many years.

A somewhat similar story was related by Paul I. Edic of
Akron, Ohio. He was using the Miracode Phonetic Index of the
1910 Federal Census of Ohio, trying to find some mention of
his ancestors who had the rather rare surname of "Huffcut."
Unfortunately, he could find no entries for the family under
any spelling variant in the index. Discouraged, he put his
work on the Huffcuts aside and decided to go ahead researching
his great uncle George A. Brewster's family instead.

However, as the phonetic index was new to him, Paul
became somewhat confused as to how the system worked and

inadvertently ordered the wrong roll of census film. As he scanned the film, the Brewsters were not to be found. But, all of a sudden, he was surprised to stumble across Frank G. Huffcut, his wife Ethel, and their family's listing in Cleveland in 1910. The handwriting on this surname had been misinterpreted and erroneously placed in the phonetic index under "Huffent," which is why Paul had not discovered it previously. He would never have found the Huffcuts had he not made that crucial mistake and requested the "wrong" roll of microfilm.

Christine Rose remembers:

"I recently was at the State Library in Nashville, Tennessee, doing client work and research on various Rose family members. I had my name down on the waiting sheet to use the microfilm copier, as I had a Hardin County will to reproduce from the original. A woman came up to me and asked if I was the 'Rose' whose name was on the sign-up sheet. I told her yes, and she explained that she too had a Rose in her background, though she had not done much work on them. I asked her in which area did they reside, and she replied that it was Wayne County. When I asked her if she remembered any of the names, she told me 'the Rose who married a Benham.'

I almost fell over! Whose will was I about to copy on the microfilm copy machine? The will of Sarah Rose, mother of Martha Rose Benham! Needless-to-say the woman was quite happy when I was able in just a few minutes to hand her the will of her ancestress. She had known nothing beyond Martha's name and did not even know they went over to Hardin County."

Myrtle Stevens Hyde of Ogden, Utah, writes:

"Aldous is one of *my* families, of which I take note whenever I see a reference. One day, while reeling a microfilm in a search for another surname, just by chance I stopped to see how the page numbers were progressing and noticed an Aldous named as a legatee in an old will. I then wrote down the will identity and the Aldous names in it.

Several years later a woman in England queried me about any knowledge of her Aldous ancestral family. The will that had 'found me' was the one that tied her to many earlier generations in another county of England from the one she already knew as an ancestral residence."

Ken D. Johnson is an expert on the revolutionary war activities of colonial residents of the Mohawk Valley in upstate New York. Ken remembers:

"Last summer I was at the Denver Archives researching films of original records of the Mohawk. I had been at the reader for three full days and was ready to quit, having examined the crucial materials many times over. But I had an unexplainable urge to review one particular film yet again, even though I had already scrutinized the parts of it that I considered to be of value at least three times before.

In order to try and escape the unpleasant feeling that I kept having, I looked once more, rolling past data on the Wemple family and into a section covering the Wendells, a group which I had no reason to believe was involved in the area at all. And there on the very end of the roll was a piece of information I had sought for years - a description of the location of the dead killed in the Fort Plank massacre. I was stunned! The children of my ancestral House and Cramer families were even listed, buried together in a mass grave four miles from Fort Plank.

If I had walked out of the library without following that weird urge and studying that last foot of film, I would never have found this piece of important information. It's another example of my view that the dead sometimes invade our minds and guide us to the objects or documents we are seeking."

Mary Jane Johns of Ventura County, California, recalls the frustrating experience of going through frame after frame of a microfilm that was poorly photographed and blurry. After plowing through ten pages of this unreadable material, all of a sudden the family data which she had been seeking for a very long time popped out on the film as clear as a bell. Upon the completion of her family's record, the microfilm once again became as indecipherable as before. But the strangest part of this story is that others checked out the same film later on and found it *all* was unreadable!

Joan Lowrey, President of the German Research

Association based in San Diego, California, remembers searching many microfilms looking for data on her ancestor Sebastian Deubel. Finally, after a long day of scanning the old records, she obtained a certain reel of film. Somewhat casually, she spun the handle of the reel forward, and it stopped on an entry that gave the long-sought-for *baptism* of her Sebastian. For some reason, she spun the handle forward again very fast - skipping many frames of film - and it stopped on her ancestor's *marriage* vital statistic. Unbelievably, she held her breath and tried one more time, turning the handle quickly and passing over many frames of film until it stopped. Yes, she had randomly spun ahead to the *burial* of her ancestor Sebastian Deubel!

Jean D. Worden went to the Fort Wayne, Indiana Library to do some searching in films of the 1851 census of Canada. She was looking for Ellen A. Conklin, her husband's great-grandmother, in any of the several counties which bordered Lake Ontario. Unlike the friends who accompanied her and took lunch and coffee breaks, the first two days Jean stubbornly stayed with the microfilm, doggedly-determined to find her elusive quarry. On the third day of unsuccessful research, the librarian told her, "The film and machine will still be here, why don't you go with your friends?" Fed up with the lack of results, Jean reluctantly agreed and went.

After enjoying a welcome break, upon her return she found a young lady sitting at the film machine beside her. The woman was in a quandary, saying, "Oh now what do I do?" Trying to be the good Samaritan, Jean helped her with her genealogical questions, especially on some New York State matters about which she was especially knowledgeable. After spending much time offering the lady advice, Jean finally returned to her own microfilm reader and her own unanswered problems. She muttered a disgusted "Oh, nuts," gave the handle a quick turn, and, lo and behold, there on the film was the entire Conklin family that she had been seeking for three days.

Maybe this "give and thou shalt receive business" has some merit to it after all!

But perhaps my favorite tale that has come in dealing with

books or microfilms is yet another story from Christine Rose. This time her husband Seymour was involved:

"When I became involved in genealogy a number of years ago, Seymour and I used to haunt the used bookstores for genealogies. One of our favorites was a bookstore in San Francisco. One day, when Seymour had to go to the City for a machine part, he passed the store and found that they had converted to paper-back books and had been selling off their inventory of used books. They had only part of one shelf left.

He walked in and idly picked a book off the shelf. He was completely surprised when it opened to a wonderfully detailed biography of his great-great grandfather Reverend Benjamin Brierly, a '49er' to California. Reverend Brierly had been born in England and immigrated to New England, and later to California. The account had all the details that one could hope for describing the trip, his life, and so many interesting details. Seymour paid $3.50 for the book and brought it home feeling, of course, elated at such a find! The amazing part of this is that the book was the fourth volume of a larger set, and was the only volume sitting on the shelf.

Of course, we shared the story more than once with others. About two years later, when showing the book to a genealogy friend, I was telling her about the story and opened the book to show it to her. Seymour was standing nearby. As I opened the book, for the first time I paid some attention to the fly leaf. I read it, and then stunned, I turned to Seymour and told him, 'Seymour, do you realize that you not only found a wonderful biography of your great-great grandfather, but that you actually *have his book?*'

The inscription, you see, was written by the compiler to his friend, the editor of the *Grass Valley Telegraph*. And, who was that editor? None other than Reverend Benjamin Brierly! Obviously, it was the reason that the book had opened to the biography, for that is where it would have been opened to most often by Reverend Brierly and his family. Seymour, I am absolutely convinced, was *meant* to have that biography!"

Christine Rose's opinion is certainly food for thought. It gives rise to an even bigger question: are we all *meant* to make certain discoveries as we climb the family tree?

# 6

# *SERENDIPITY & THE OPTIMIST'S CLUB*

I've always considered myself a "lucky" genealogist. Many times, while looking for something else, I've unexpectedly "stumbled" over a crucial name or date that I needed to complete a family pedigree. Because of this, I am constantly amazed at my own good fortune.

Others share my delight and this gift! The late Dr. Kenn Stryker-Rodda, one of the true "greats" of American genealogy, gave a rousing talk at a National Genealogical Society banquet in the early 1980s entitled "Ralph Smith & Of The Three Crucial Episodes In My Pursuit Of Him," a tape of which was passed on to me by Rabbi Malcolm H. Stern. Kenn delighted the crowd with his views and genealogical experiences and even gave a brief history of the term "serendipity:"

"Horace Walpole (1717 - 1797) wrote of the 'Three Princes of Serendip,' who in their travels were always coming upon, by chance or sagacity, goals that they were not in quest of. Hence, he created the word 'serendipity' based on Serendip. Now although I have never found the word 'serendipity' in a genealogical dictionary, and I think that most writers on the subject disregard it, I'm certain that almost as many cases are solved by serendipity as by ratiocination (logical reasoning)."

Kenn then went on to detail the three fortunate discoveries that enabled him to fully document the origins of his elusive Ralph Smith. The first happy find came in the Old Manuscript Room of the New Jersey Historical Society when he was not looking for Ralph at all, but for the Todd family. The second unexpected discovery on Smith was when he was looking for Ruloffsen data at the parsonage of the Old Zion Lutheran

Church in Oldwick, New Jersey. Ralph "shouldn't" have been in the records there as he was a Presbyterian. But when the Lutheran Pastor pulled out some old 18th-century leases written in Ralph Smith's distinctive hand, and there on the reverse side of one was a complete list of Smith's 13 children and their places of birth, Kenn said he couldn't help yelling out, "I found the bastard!" The third incident happened in his office, as he was examining a membership application for the Flagon & Trencher Society (of which he was co-founder) and not thinking about Ralph Smith at all. A woman presented her application, appending to it a copy of a 1764 deed. The document just happened to contain references to the hitherto-unknown earlier residence of Ralph Smith's family and enabled Kenn to finally trace his ancestry.

After relating his remarkable tale, Kenn then remarked to his audience,

> "I hereby announce my candidacy to be the *Fourth* Prince of Serendip with full rights to the practice of serendipity!"

Carol Willsey Bell had been corresponding with an historical society in Lawrence, Kansas after discovering they had an extensive collection of photos on a branch of her Bushong family. They sent her a list of identified photographs in their collection, among which was one titled "William Brubaker, Grandma Bushong's brother." Carol knew that "Grandma" was Adaline Brubaker, who had married William Bushong in Shenandoah County, Virginia, and then moved to Columbiana County, Ohio. She relates,

> "I proceeded to order copies of most of the pictures in the collection, including William Brubaker. While awaiting their arrival, I rented a roll of film of the *Alliance Standard Review*, published in a neighboring county. Due to its proximity to Columbiana County, I knew it would have items of interest. I chose a roll at random, with no particular object in mind.
>
> Imagine my amazement when I *stumbled* across the obituary of William Brubaker, in which mention was made of his nephew, Peter Bushong of Columbiana. I had absolutely no idea of WHERE this man lived or in which

time period he had died! A week later, the photograph arrived, a wonderful picture of him in his civil war uniform. The doors had opened on all fronts all at once."

In another instance, Carol was working on a family group sheet for a civil war soldier, Jonas Harrold. From census, she had determined that he had four sons. Data could be found on three, but not the fourth son. She recalls:

"Setting the sheet aside, I started to read newspaper articles on microfilm, continuing my project of carefully abstracting all death and marriage notices from Columbiana County, Ohio newspapers. In the third issue, I *stumbled* across the marriage of Harmon Harrold to Laura Buckley in the 1893 newspaper I was reading. Voila!"

Nick Vine Hall has had many interesting experiences along these lines:

"I once strangely 'tripped over' a 1930's newspaper account, which quoted extracts of a passenger's diary on a voyage to South Australia from England in 1850 aboard the ship *Agincourt*. My ancestor, Mary Small, was on that ship, and I was able to learn all about her voyage. The MOST curious thing about this story is that the newspaper cutting was in a vast series of about 30,000 ships' pictures collection at the Mitchell Library in Sydney, and it was next to a picture of the Orient line steamer *S.S. Chimborazo*, of which my great-grandfather, Captain John Vine Hall (1845-1932) was the master in the 1870's. All of the other items seemed to be arranged in alphabetical order by the name of the ship, and there was no catalogue card entry for the *Agincourt* item. What is even more curious, is that there was no connection, that I know of, between the Hall and Small families until my mother married my father in 1943!"

Brenda Dougall Merriman was looking for data on a man committed to a lunatic asylum in the 1840s. She searched various census lists, available jail and mental health registers, land and tax records, and cemeteries with no success. Then, by sheer chance while reading census lists for a different client in a totally unrelated area, Brenda found the wife of the lunatic along with families of his two married daughters and even another child. She would never have discovered this important information on a "normal," logical hunt, as the geographic locale of the census was far off the beaten path from where the family supposedly resided!

This sort of thing has happened several times in her research. In another instance, Brenda was investigating a client's female ancestor, born in 1862, orphaned at age 9, who was raised (said tradition) by an aunt. Brenda looked and looked for documented data, but found little. Then, while working for another client on a totally unrelated case, she was scanning local newspapers. Again, as she says "*by sheer chance*," Brenda discovered the long-sought-for woman's parents being arrested in early 1871 for operating a house of ill fame. As the article suggested that they probably soon went to jail, this can explain why they were unrecorded in the census later that year and were so difficult to trace! The child eventually was rescued and protected by her aunt.

Quite a story!

Marie Martin Murphy of Bartlett, Illinois, recalls:

"There have been many times when I was looking for something else entirely and have come across what I needed. I remember a long search for the evidence of the first husband of a woman in Shelby County, Kentucky. There was an abundance of information about her second husband, but nothing to indicate who her first husband had been. I had searched every available record I could think of with absolutely no success. I had gone over the deed indexes with a fine tooth comb with no luck whatsoever. So I had finally written my client and told her that the proof just wasn't available.

Two weeks later, working on a completely different family, I was flipping through an early deed book looking for the page I required. For some reason, I stopped to read one of the pages as I was about to pass it by. There on that page was a deposition for the settlement of an early land grant - and the man giving the deposition was the son of the man I had been searching for. He gave the date the man who was claiming the land arrived in Shelby County, and said that he (the deponent) remembered it well because he had been there since before the claimant arrived. In the process of explaining who he was, he mentioned his mother, the widow of 'John Doe' - and bingo! There was the information I had been searching for. And since the deponents were not listed in the index, I would never have found it without reading every word of every deed book.

Now why in the world did I flip open just that page, and why in the world did I stop to read it! As anyone knows who does genealogy for pay, you just can't stop and read odd pages as you go along, or your clients would be rightfully upset. I have no logical explanation - other than serendipity .. or magic!"

### Myrtle Stevens Hyde observes:

"Years ago, before computers helped us, I found in the Putney, Vermont Town Records the publication of the marriage of my ancestor, Seth Drake, in 1784. His bride-to-be was 'Chloe Printess of Warwick.' Studying maps, I found no Warwick in Vermont, but eventually found one south of Vermont in Massachusetts. And yes, the vital records were on microfilm in Salt Lake City. The records even had an index, and I easily found Seth Drake's name. There the good fortune ended. The actual listed page contained no Seth Drake. 'Now I'll have to go through this whole film to find him,' I said to myself resignedly. And so I began. But before Seth and Chloe's entry appeared, I found the birth of an ancestor of my husband's whom we previously had no idea resided in Warwick! Pondering the circumstance of the entry in the index, I felt that someone long before was 'guided' to write down that wrong page number so that I would find the people I wasn't seeking."

### Nils William Olsson of Winter Park, Florida, remembers:

"I have been sorting out my own experiences and, to be sure, there are times when one hits upon a lucky break; but I have always felt that this was more or less happenstance. In my own family, I have a great-great-great grandfather who left Stockholm in the early years of the 19th century, destination unknown. He must have died before 1825, since his deserted wife died in that year and is listed as a widow.

But what happened to the old man? Since there are well over 2,000 parishes in Sweden, it was unthinkable of wading through all of those parish registers to find him, so I decided that was one antecedent for whom I had no death date. Then one day as I was doing entirely different research, my ancient grandfather's name popped out on the page. Sure enough, there he was, with his death date and his place of death. Now what would you call this? Luck? Hunch? Instinct? I leave that to you!"

Apropos of this while I was mulling over all these stories, Dr. Helen Hinchliff of Fulford Harbour, Canada, and Dr. William B. ("Bart") Saxbe, Jr. of Oberlin, Ohio, each sent me the same relevant quotation by Louis Pasteur. Their letters "happened" to arrive at my San Diego post office box on the same day, giving their message a double-whammy impact. (Bart actually was writing me from far away Miraj, India, where he was temporarily assisting at a mission hospital there). They both thought it important that Pasteur had said, *"In the field of study, chance favors only the prepared mind."*

Bart Saxbe goes on to comment:

"Genealogical successes are born of skill, perseverance, and luck. Luck is especially important early in a researcher's career, in the interval between the development of curiosity and the development of competence. I suspect that most committed genealogists have had some early success which produced such a 'rush' of surprise and joy that they got permanently hooked. In spite of the boredom and frustration which are our usual fare, the sweet recollection of triumph lingers on to keep the addiction alive.

It is a common belief that scientists - or inventors or explorers - use conscious reasoning to achieve their ends. In fact, we have a very poor understanding of the process of discovery, which frequently involves irrational or unconscious leaps of intuition. If we ascribe our good results to intuition, we claim possession of a valuable talent, one that might be cultivated. But who can disprove the role of luck, serendipity, fate, coincidence, or divine grace, for none of which do we receive credit? Some will deny that any of these 'gifts' exist. I do not know, but I have my own disprovable opinion: I do concur with Dr. Pasteur that chance favors only the prepared mind."

Helen Hinchliff remarks:

"I agree with Louis Pasteur. Serendipity is rarely the result of mere good luck. It happens because we are *prepared* to see and to understand what lies before our eyes. As an example, on a recent trip to London, my husband Donald Simmons and I were looking for the site of John Simmons and Company, Wholesale Stationers, once at 59 Bishopsgate Without. It started to rain, and we headed for the nearest door we could find, which turned out to be the Bishopsgate Institute. Not only did its librarian tell us that we were standing almost directly on the site of John Simmon's place of business, but the library's rare book collection contained an artist's sketchbook of nineteenth-century watercolor drawings of every place of business on Bishopsgate Without. Among them was a drawing of 'John Simmons and Company.'

You may consider our discovery of this book extraordinary luck, and it is. I contend, however, that it was not merely the result of good luck. We follow a number of basic principles of research, and many of our serendipitous discoveries are, in the end, attributable to the fact that when we do field research, we are prepared!"

One of the basic principles to which Helen refers is having the right mental attitude. She notes:

"Many beginning genealogists tell me that they cannot find anything interesting about their ancestors. Indeed, some admit they think their forebears are boring. Nonsense! Every ancestor lived a full, probably richly interesting life, if you could but find the facts. If you adopt the attitude that each of your ancestors is potentially interesting - if you only knew more about them - then you are prepared to start the search for the documents through which their lives can be revealed."

Bart Saxbe writes:

"I am a genealogist, but I support my family by my work

as a surgeon. Surgeons have a saying which genealogists will appreciate: 'It's better to be lucky than good.' Do not misunderstand: I am a good surgeon and a good genealogist, but I am frequently lucky too. Sometimes I have orthonoia, the opposite of paranoia: the belief that, behind my back and without my knowledge, people and events are secretly conspiring to do things for my benefit. Records pop up where I would not expect them, long-lost relatives answer my letters and phone calls, civil servants volunteer help, and unlikely contacts produce unsought documents.

For example, I once gave a talk to a county genealogical society in northwestern Ohio on the subject of preponderance of evidence, and used, for an illustration, a local Snider family I had been researching with minimal returns. A week later, an attendee wrote me to offer a Snider family Bible that had just been found in an abandoned house. It turned out to be *the* family Bible of my Sniders, and it contained excellent primary data and leads found nowhere else!"

### Hazel C. Patrick of Herkimer, New York, comments:

"When I am working on a family, I try to relate to them. I have feelings that something may be right or wrong, and the 'hunch' turns out usually to be right. I often open a book while looking for something, and it opens to the right page. *I look hopefully*, and I find information where it has no reason to be!"

### Dr. Raymond M. Bell of Washington, Pennsylvania, writes:

"Is it a 'sixth sense' that, when in a library, you sometimes seem to know to look in unlikely places? A friend of mine went to our local courthouse and found something for which I had been searching. She did not know it was not there, so she looked and found it! I knew it could not be there (the man died in another county), so I did not look.

Here lies a lesson! One of my genealogical rules is *Don't give up!* It may take twenty years, but keep searching. Pretend that you are Sherlock Holmes and try to use his methods. The answers are there waiting for you to find them."

Helen Hinchliff thinks Dr. Bell has a very important point. She observes:

"We need to learn to be open to the possibility that our ancestors *will* be mentioned in books that seem unlikely. I had never checked *Scottish Notes and Queries* for anyone in Helen Law's family, because I considered them to have been too insignificant for anyone to have noted or queried. When the librarian in the Special Collections Department at the Aberdeen University Library suggested I look there for Duncan Law, Helen's father, I pooh-poohed the idea. Nevertheless, he persevered, and I looked over his shoulder. My eye saw 'Duncan Law,' and I exclaimed, 'There he is!' The librarian looked at me as if I were the most naive victim of the 'he's got the same name, so he must be the same man syndrome.' But we looked up the entry anyway. It was an item in the abstracted apprenticeship records of 17th century Aberdeen. Still, I was wrong. He wasn't Helen's father; he was her grandfather! Further, the information in the record pointed the way to her great-grandfather."

I totally agree with my colleagues. To put it bluntly, pessimists make lousy genealogists. If I've learned one thing over the years it's that a positive mind-set is essential when climbing the family tree. To ensure success, we all have to think and behave like charter members of the Optimist Club!

# 7
# *RESEARCH ON SUNDAY*

In 1959, the late Donald Lines Jacobus, acknowledged "Dean of American Genealogists" and pioneer in our "scientific approach" to family history, published an article by Winifred Lovering Holman, entitled "Randall-Pease-Hutchinson-Warner: A Study In Serendipity" in his prestigious magazine *The American Genealogist*. Mrs. Holman's interesting study told of the unusual chain of events that eventually led her to successful identification of these old Massachusetts families. In her article, she defined serendipity as "the happy faculty of finding or accomplishing things without direct or conscious effort."

The many letters from my colleagues echo Winifred Holman's experience. Some show that serendipitous discoveries in genealogical research often are of the gentlest sort, in the "non-earthshaking" variety. An example of this would be the fortuitous stumbling over a query in a genealogical column, something that seems to happen quite often. For instance, David P. Hively of Red Lion, Pennsylvania, owes his success in documenting his ancestor Benjamin Franklin *Lighty*, supposedly a soldier for the *Union* side in the civil war, to chancing upon a request for information in a periodical sent in (as a "long shot") by someone looking for data on his forefather Benjamin F. *Lidy*, a *Confederate* marine! Yes, correspondence and then investigation proved they were one and the same man (who may have fought on both sides during the rebellion!).

Other serendipitous genealogical experiences can be a bit more jarring - and they don't necessarily have to occur within the confines of a library or archive where we usually would expect them. For often - if we are prepared, open, and enthusiastic - my colleagues attest that we can find our ancestors *outside* the normal research facilities and repositories, anyday ... anywhere ... anytime!

Janet Worthington of Sydney, Australia, writes:

"I have the utmost respect for what I call 'the unknown dimension' or the source of unexpected and unexplicable information. About four years ago, I received a tape recording in the mail from my Kent (England) researcher. She had never sent a tape recording before; usually, she sent snips of paper with family references she had found during her searches for a number of clients. As I listened to this tape, I could not believe my ears as it recorded briefly the contents of nine old original documents, including my very own ancestor's wills and deeds covering a timespan between 1730 and 1830.

A neighbour of my researcher had casually passed by a second-hand dealer who was displaying his wares at a Saturday morning fair. On a trestle table, he noticed an old parchment will with the name 'Worthington' on it. When he returned home, he told my researcher of his find. She happened to be home that morning, which was unusual for her on a Saturday, so she jumped in her car and drove several miles to the town where the fair was being held. The parchment was one of several which were found in the bottom of a box of old china. The papers had been sitting around his house for ten years prior to the decision to display one document that day at the fair. She bargained with the dealer and bought the lot. The papers are now safely stored with me here in Australia."

Fate was certainly on my side that day. The chances of this happening, I think, are as great as winning the lottery!

A very similar occurrence involved my friends Mary K. Meyer and Annette K. Burgert. As Mary relates:

"A couple of years ago, Annette went up to Easton, Pennsylvania, or some nearby place to give a lecture. That day there was an ephemera show in the same town, but she could not attend because of her previous commitment. Instead, she sent her husband Dick over to the show with instructions to buy "X" number of dollars worth of any original documents written in German. She went to her meeting, and Dick dutifully attended the ephemera show.

The next morning, Annette was examining the previous day's purchases. She looked carefully at the old German script, laboriously translating the material to see what bearing it might have on her great interest in early German immigrants of Pennsylvania. One document she examined was a 1792 deed in English, but with a signature in German script which she translated as 'Frederick Agler.' She recognized the name as that of one of my ancestors for whom I had been searching for some forty years. Annette's first thought was, 'Well, this is really strange that Mary never found this deed before. Surely she must have searched the Dauphin County, Pennsylvania deeds for the elusive Frederick.' The next time Annette went to Harrisburg, she checked at the courthouse ... and would you believe ... the deed had never been recorded!

Did the Great God of Genealogy have a hand in the preservation of this deed for 200 years? Did he guide Annette's husband to purchase it at the ephemera show and preserve in Annette's computer-like mind this man's name? Did his hand bring it home to me after 200 years - to me, the person who would value it above all else? Or was it coincidental, dumb, stupid luck? Who knows! But thanks to this marvelous find and its contents, I now know the name of Frederick Agler's father!"

James Owen Schuyler of San Carlos, California, took a genealogical trip to the British Isles in 1988. While researching his Owen and Roberts forefathers on the Island of Anglesey in the north part of Wales, he had the opportunity to visit the church at Amlwch in the heart of his ancestral locale. Jim recalls:

"We met the junior warden there as he was replastering one of the church walls. We told him about the research we were doing, and he suggested that we walk down the street and see Margaret Hughes, a lady who runs a yarn shop and is very much interested in the genealogy of the Amlwch people. Margaret was in her shop when we got there, and I told her about my ancestor William Owen and his uncle

William Roberts. I promised to send her two papers that I had prepared on them when I got back to the States.

When we arrived home in San Carlos about a month later, there was a letter waiting for me from Margaret! She wrote that she had been ironing one evening and, for some reason, thought about an old diary that had been found on a trash heap during World War II which was rescued by a man interested in Amlwch history. She thought she remembered an entry in the diary about two men going to California. She put down the ironing board, got the diary, and found the following two entries:

*'22 April 1859, William Roberts and William Owens, the shop, go by steamer to Liverpool and California.'*

*'27 April 1859, William Roberts and William Owens, the shop, start from Liverpool to California.'*

She had found my ancestor! A later check of their ages in a passenger list confirmed the find!"

Nick Vine Hall has had many discoveries that qualify as serendipitous. He recently had a client who was a descendant of one William Douglas, an Irish farmer, and his wife Ann Cody who lived at Paisley, Scotland in 1814. This research case had ground to a halt after four years, because of the very common surname and lack of available indexed records for Ireland. Investigations in the normal repositories seemed at a dead end. Suddenly the descendant remembered that he possessed an old family watch in his safe, inscribed "John Douglas, Glasgow, 1867." When asked, his old mother remarked, "Oh, that belonged to a relative of your father's who was a sea captain lost off the west coast of Scotland." Nick recalls,

"In a blinding flash of inspiration, I decided to check *Lloyd's Captain's Register, 1869*. There were eight 'John Douglas' entries, after one of which were the words 'Lost October 26, 1868.' The book then gave a fully detailed history of the Captain's life and vital statistics, including the facts that he was born in 1822 in Ardrossan, Scotland, only 32 miles from Glasgow, and was lost in 1868 off the west coast of Scotland (just one year after the date inscribed on the old watch). It seems pretty likely that we have found the right John Douglas. Who knows where this clue will now lead us?"

John C. McCornack of Peoria, Illinois certainly has an incredible tale to tell:

"During a recent business trip to Europe, I ended up with my friend, Tom Adams, in Manchester, England. We had a free weekend, so we decided to rent a BMW and drove up to the Newton Stewart area of Scotland to make a first-time visit to my ancestral homes.

The trip was a great success. We spent Saturday roaming around the country and were lucky enough to find homes, named Annabaglish and Barwinnock, where my McCornack ancestors lived before they came to Illinois in the 1830's. Everywhere we went we asked, 'Do you know or have you known a McCornack?' The answer was always the same, 'No!' By noon Saturday, we decided it was time to return to England. Tom drove the BMW, and I settled down to reflect on my rewarding experiences in McCornack country. In my possession were about 150 pictures and four hours of tape recordings documenting my trip. But little did I know that the best was yet to come.

As we traveled for about 100 miles through various towns, we noticed that most of the stores were closed because it was Sunday. Tom expressed concern that the trip was nearing the end, and he had not yet bought his wife a gift. As we approached one of the last towns in Scotland, Tom suddenly pulled the BMW to a stop beside a store which was open. We were greeted by a young sales lady. Before long Tom was selecting a hand-knit sweater. After looking at the quality of the sweaters, I decided that my wife should also have one. We made our purchases and were about to leave when Tom noticed his sweater did not have a label. He asked the sales lady, 'How am I going to convince anyone this is a hand-knit sweater from Scotland?' By this time the clerk's mother had come out of a back room and said, 'No problem, we will sew a label in the sweater.' She took both sweaters to a back room, and shortly returned with labels in the sweaters that read ...

---'I AM A McCORNACK'---

I am a McCornack!

Continuing the conversation, Tom mentioned that we had been over in the Newton Stewart area doing genealogical research on the McCornacks. The lady stopped and said, 'I am a McCornack!' I tried to reassure her that she may be a McCormack or McCormick, but she was not a McCornack because we spelled our name differently. She said, 'No! I *am* a McCornack!' and ran to the back room to pick up her purse. From her purse she pulled a well-worn letter. It was a letter dated 1946 written to her mother, Agnes Fraser, from Richard McCornack (who died in 1959). During World War II, Richard had made written contact with what is now believed to be the last McCornack family in Scotland. The families in Scotland had a rough time during the war, and Richard and his family had provided much-needed food and clothing parcels. The lady's mother had given her the letter and had told her, 'Keep this letter, and someday a McCornack will come to see you!'

So it was on this late Sunday afternoon that a descendant of Andrew McCornack who left Scotland in 1839 made the first known personal contact with a member of the McCornack family that stayed in Scotland. There is no way the odds could be figured on this chance occurrence which happened over eighty miles from the ancestral area. It is an example of what makes the search for our ancestors such a rewarding experience! Letter exchanges continued, the hand-knit sweater business was renamed, and as a result 'McCornack Country' labeled hand-knit sweaters are now available throughout the world."

**Stephen Samuel Barthel of West Jordan, Utah, had an experience he will never forget:**

"One of the first people I met after starting to research my ancestry was Lloyd E. Miesen, Sr. of Portland Oregon. He had sent my Great Aunt Amelia a nine-generation chart of the Miesen family, giving full names, dates and places of those people on it. Lloyd had been doing genealogical research since the 1930's, and promised all those he interviewed that he would share the information with anyone who was interested.

While I was on a two year mission for my church in Germany, Lloyd put me in contact with a second cousin named Tom Boles of Mesquite, Texas. Tom was gathering data on the descendant families of our immigrant ancestor Peter Miesen and had assembled over 600 family group sheets. But Tom was quite ill, and wrote me that his chances appeared dismal for a recovery from a severe heart problem. Feeling a sense of urgency in getting together with Tom and examining those important genealogical papers, I flew from Germany to see him, arriving in America on 22nd November, 1972.

But the same evening I arrived, I received a late-night phone call from Tom Boles. He told me not to come to his home, as it was no longer there. A tornado had destroyed his trailer the night before and most of the contents. The *only* thing left on the cement slab was the manuscript to the 600+ family group sheets. To us it was a miracle!

We eventually met, and Tom promised me that if anything should happen to him prior to publishing the manuscript, I was to get the records. Tom was Presbyterian, but he knew how important the genealogy was to me, because of my membership in the L.D.S. Church. He knew I would take good care of it.

I continued to spend time gathering data on the Miesens, sharing much information with Lloyd Miesen who eventually published the book for Tom Boles in 1973. I lost contact with Tom while attending school, but I shall never forget him. When the Social Security Death Index was made available through the L.D.S. Family History Library, I checked it and found that Tom had passed away in 1980. I have been using that Index to see when others noted in the Miesen volume might have died and have computerized the names in the book for the Ancestral File. All this information is now readily available to those using the Family History Center. I'm trying to continue the promise of help that Lloyd made to the old timers when he started his research back in the 1930's."

Dr. Helen Hinchliff had another exhilarating instance of serendipitous discovery:

"On one of our trips devoted solely to my German Mumper family research, my husband Donald and I stopped briefly to visit my birthplace, Rockford Illinois. My mother was a Californian; my father, a Rockford native. When they married out west, he took her home to meet his family. They returned to California when I was eight months old, so I did not know my birthplace at all. Further, I had done relatively little research on my father's Emerson and Talcott ancestors. About all I knew was that they had settled in Rockford in the early 1830's and had become industrialists.

We arrived in Rockford on a Sunday morning when all the record offices were closed. That did not matter because we had not intended doing research on this branch of my family. It was enough to photograph the Emerson wing of the Rockford Hospital, which had been named after my great-great grandfather, Ralph Emerson, and where my father, Ralph Hinchliff, Jr., and I had been born. We found the hospital, but the building was not old enough to have served as my birthplace, let alone my father's. Instead of driving on to the next town on our route, I went in to ask directions to the old hospital. The very young receptionist reported that it had long since been torn down, but that the Rockford Museum Center had a replica which we might like to view.

At the Museum Center, I learned that while it was true that the hospital in which I was born was gone, their replica was of Rockford's very first hospital, a structure built in the mid-nineteenth century for a small, frontier town. Undeterred, I revised my goal and wondered whether the museum might hold anything at all about my ancestors. Ralph Emerson owned a factory which had produced reapers and carriages, among other things; further, he had owned the Burson Knitting Company of which my grandfather, Ralph Hinchliff, Sr., had been a director. The hostess replied happily that the museum featured examples of some Emerson farm equipment; but something more exciting was in store: at that very moment the Burson Knitting Company was holding an open house across town. We could tour the factory!

Donald and I agreed. We cashed in our museum tickets and raced across town to see the factory. When we arrived, I introduced myself to the guide at the entrance and was disappointed to learn that this was the Nelson Knitting Company; Burson's had long since gone out of business and the buildings torn down. We wanted to see the old knitting machines anyway, so we got into line. As we stood there I gave Donald a brief rundown on my Rockford ancestors; I could see ears perking up around me as I mentioned names and dates. It was not long before the couple immediately preceding us in line introduced themselves. We were standing behind the best man at the wedding of one of my uncles. About ten minutes later, the tour guide came up to report the arrival of a very elderly Mr. Nelson (who had been the son of my grandfather's friendly competitor). Mr. Nelson was delightful, and one of his anecdotes about my grandfather provided some insight into why we were touring the Nelson - rather than the Burson - Knitting Company. It seems my grandfather spent a bit too much of his time playing golf.

We were inspired to take an extra day at the city library and were leaving town Tuesday morning, the last possible day if we were to maintain our schedule. At the last minute, we decided to return to the museum; it would take less than an hour to see the Emerson farm equipment. Upon entering, I introduced myself to the receptionist, and reported the wonderful experience we had at the Nelson open house. I also mentioned my family names again. Then Donald and I proceeded to the industrial wing. It was not long before the museum director came forward with some excitement to report that this was the first day of a new exhibit on period costumes of Rockford, and that I was in for a treat. He then conducted us to an exhibit featuring a petite mannequin - only size 6 - who was wearing the dress worn by Adaline Elizabeth Talcott the day she married Ralph Emerson in 1858. How's that for learning about your great-great grandmother in a new and different way?

We finally took a look at the Emerson industrial exhibit and were about to leave when Donald noticed a press photographer preparing to take a picture of Adaline's dress. Donald thought perhaps his photographs would be of better quality than mine. Never leaving a stone unturned, I strode up to him, introduced myself and my relationship to the woman who had once worn the wedding dress and asked whether I might be able to purchase one of his photographs. Before I knew it, he was taking my photograph standing beside her. It was absolutely thrilling, almost as if I were being photographed with my ancestor. The photograph, together with an interview

Photo by Don Holt/*The Registar Star*

Helen Hinchliff & her great-great-grandmother's wedding dress.

with Donald and me, appeared in the *Rockford Register Star* on 17 September 1988. By then we were already in Pennsylvania, but when we returned home I had received a letter from my grandfather's former personal secretary!

The entire experience is almost incredible. The timing was uncanny. We arrived precisely in time for the Nelson Knitting Company's annual open house, itself an unusual occurrence. By taking the tour and meeting people who had known my family, we were inspired to spend a day in the library, something which was completely unplanned and which produced a treasure trove of material. This, in turn, motivated us to return to the museum and see the Emerson exhibit. Our reward was to visit the museum on the first day it would have been possible to see Adaline's dress!

What lessons can I draw from this experience? Certainly, Donald and I were in the right place at the right time. But it is also true that being interested in my ancestors *as people* - rather than merely as names and dates on a pedigree chart - was a major factor in my having met my uncle's best man, chatted with my grandfather's friendly competitor, received a letter from his personal secretary, and experienced the closest approximation one can possibly have to being photographed with one's youthful great-great grandmother!

# 8
# SYNCHRONICITY:
# YOU MAKE ME FEEL SO JUNG

Many of the intriguing incidents you have just read about would fall under the category of being a "synchronicity," a term coined by the eminent psychologist Carl Jung. He defined synchronicity as a meaningful coincidence without apparent cause which has value for the person who experiences it.

Jung had a classic illustration of this kind of event himself which occurred during therapy. His patient, a young woman whose highly rational approach to life made treatment exceedingly difficult, related a dream in which a golden scarab beetle appeared. Jung was aware that this insect had great significance as a symbol of rebirth to the ancient Egyptian culture. As the woman was speaking, Jung heard a tapping on the window of the room. He opened it, and in flew a greenish-gold colored scarab. From that moment on, as the beetle's appearance had a special meaning to the patient, the woman's rigidly rational view of life was pierced, and her sessions with Dr. Jung blossomed and became much more productive. Jung felt that synchronicities such as this often were outer manifestations of inner transformations and turbulence.

In my own life, the death of singer Elvis Presley in 1977 gave me a similar incident to ponder. Elvis (interestingly enough a direct descendant of one of my beloved Palatine 1709ers, Valentin[1] Pressler) had been an important and formative influence on my early musical career, from my high school rock-and-roll group days on. I had even patterned my very early singing efforts after his distinctive style, so enamored was I of his exciting sound. You can imagine my delight then, when after years of pounding the pavement in Hollywood trying to obtain a recording contract, in 1961 Presley's own producer, Steve Sholes, finally signed me and my partner Dean Kay to RCA Victor Records, Elvis's label. Several of Elvis's key band members played on our sessions, and it was a thrill to record with them and be marketed in the RCA advertising packages with "The King."

After I went into acting, the budding association continued. My very first motion picture role was in MGM's "Girl Happy," starring Elvis. I had just a bit part in the film, but Presley couldn't have been nicer to me. He was every inch the southern gentleman and a pleasure to work with. Elvis was truly in his prime then and seemed to have the whole world at his command. So it was especially sad to see his gradual disintegration from the effects of prescription drugs and the pressures of super-stardom in the years that followed. When he passed away, I was devastated and felt a sense of personal loss.

When CBS-TV broadcast his last filmed concert performance on October 3, 1977, I almost couldn't bring myself to watch it. The evening the special was aired was traumatic for me. I was so emotionally distraught and grieved at the loss and waste of such a good man, the tears were flowing even before the program began. As I sat back in my chair, stressed out but determined somehow to watch Elvis's final appearance, I felt an unknown energy, almost an electricity, pulsing throughout my living room. It was so strong I could almost touch it. Then at the very mini-second the show began, a large, framed picture of my daughter hanging on the wall opposite my chair crashed to the floor with a gigantic boom. In all my years of living in that house, no picture had ever fallen and none ever did again.

I've thought and thought about that incident many times since then, its exact and precise timing as the concert started, my state of mind at that moment, and especially the profound sense of grief I was feeling. To most others, it would have been just a picture falling off the wall, an occurrence of no real import. To my mind, then and now however, it was a true synchronicity - a coincidence involving internal and external events which had a very special meaning only to me.

For the rest of the entire evening I had the eerie feeling that an unseen presence was with me during that concert. It was uncanny and downright spooky. I can't help remembering that at the end of every Presley public appearance, an announcer would always get on the p.a. system and close the show by announcing, "Elvis has left the building." In my home the night of October 3, 1977, I wasn't so sure that he had!

I have found that the literature relating to synchronicity is absolutely fascinating. One of the best books in the field is Arthur Koestler's classic and widely acclaimed *The Roots of Coincidence*. As another fine writer, Alan Vaughan, remarks, "(Koestler's book) compares the perversity of physics with the equally perverse data of parapsychology and finds they meet in synchronicity." Mr. Koestler's study confined itself mostly to the experimental results of laboratory research and of the pioneers who conducted it. For example, he detailed the experiments of physicist Paul Kammerer dealing with laws of Seriality, and his attempts to prove that coincidences, whether they come singly or in series, are manifestations of a universal principle in nature that operates independently from physical causation. Kammerer also believed that co-existent with causality, the principle that nothing can exist without a cause, is an *a-causal* principle active in the universe which tends towards unity. He felt that seriality was the umbilical cord that connects thought, feeling, science, and art with the womb of the universe that gave birth to them!

Another great physicist of similar bent was Wolfgang Pauli. Koestler describes Pauli's work and sets forth his belief in non-causal, non-physical factors operating in nature. Pauli, in addressing the mysteries of ESP and other such phenomena, felt it was hopeless to explain them in normal cause and effect terms, and preferable and more honest to accept that parapsychological phenomena, including apparent coincidences, were the visible traces of untraceable a-causal principles in the universe. This view and others like it led physicist Sir James Jeans to comment in one of his Rede Lectures, "The stream of knowledge is heading towards a non-mechanical reality; the universe begins to look more like a great thought than like a great machine."

As if to show unity between their two fields, Pauli's essay on Kepler was published together with Carl Jung's treatise on *Synchronicity: An Acausal Connecting Principle* first in German in 1952 and then in English in 1955. As Arthur Koestler notes, "It was for the first time in the history of modern thought that the hypothesis of a-causal factors working in the universe was given the joint stamp of respectability by a psychologist and a physicist of international renown." In his essay, Jung postulated that synchronicity affects our lives just as much as logical reality does, being  an underlying principle of the universe as important as physical cause and effect. He cites, among other things, ESP, prophetic dreams, psychokinesis, déjà vu, unconscious foreknowledge, and Seriality as manifestations of this via the unconscious mind.

An informative and entertaining book, full of pertinent case histories along these lines, is Alan Vaughan's *Incredible Coincidence: The Baffling World of Synchronicity.* Typical of the examples he sets forth is his Case #2, entitled "Cabin Boy Cannibalism," a story that won a "Coincidence Competition" in the *Sunday Times* of London in 1974. It concerned a horrific fictional story written by Edgar Allan Poe in the mid-19th century about three shipwreck survivors in an open boat who killed and ate the fourth, a cabin boy whose name was Richard Parker. Some years later, as confirmed by the *Times* report of the ensuing murder trial, three shipwreck survivors in an open boat *actually* killed and ate the fourth, a cabin boy whose name *was* Richard Parker! Vaughan also details the odd and very strange manner in which this tale was brought to his attention - full of synchronistic events too.

Another example is Case #5, "A Chance Accident," in which motorcyclist Frederick Chance collided with a car being driven by none other than Frederick Chance in 1973 at Stourbridge, England. Then there is Case #39, "Pinching Yourself," when Mr. George D. Bryson made a spontaneous decision while mid-trip on a train to get off at Louisville, Kentucky, just because he had never seen the city before. He inquired at the station as to a nice place to stay, and was directed to the Brown Hotel. When he registered, as a total lark, he inquired if there was any mail waiting for him. The desk clerk calmly handed him a letter addressed to "Mr. George D. Bryson, Room 307," that being the number of the room to which he had just been assigned. It turned out that the preceding resident of Room 307 was another George D. Bryson, an insurance agent from Montreal.

Each and every case Vaughan presents is intriguing, some even quite poignant and moving. Case #109, "The Nature Of Love," is one of the latter. It concerns Christopher Hegarty and the portent that led to his second marriage. He was very fond of a certain lady he had been dating, but both he and Marian were reluctant to enter into marriage again. One evening, an unread book on his bookshelf somehow stood out and invited him to read it. Titled *The Nature of Love*, it discussed the writings of Kahlil Gibran, author of *The Prophet*. The section "Marriage" struck him as particularly apt, saying that some marriages are intended to end, while others are sacred. Christopher telephoned Marian and read her the passages. Marian gasped and told him that she was holding the same book in her hands, had underlined the same passages he had read, and was going to read them to him! As they compared notes, they discovered that both of them had read one other section of the book, "Love." Neither he nor she knew the other had even heard of the book.

This startling omen they took to mean that marriage was not only possible but that it would be sacred. At their wedding ceremony in Pennsylvania, the minister read the passage from *The Prophet* that was discussed in *The Nature of Love*. Hegarty winked at Marian, thinking that she had arranged this with the minister. She squeezed his hand, thinking that he had arranged it, and said, "Thank you, honey. That was very touching."

Then they realized that neither one of them had talked to the minister. The wedding had been arranged through his office, and they first met him at the wedding. The minister had no way of knowing that that particular passage on marriage had been the omen that tied their knot of love. Synchronistically, the minister had chosen the passage that had particular meaning for them. And still does.

As you can see, synchronistic events contributed by my genealogical associates fill this book. Some are such pure examples of the genre they could be included in Alan Vaughan's study. For instance, one of my dear friends is David Martin, a highly-skilled family historian who recently retired from his job as an English teacher at the local high school in West Chazy, New York. A few years ago while searching for the ancestral home of his forebears James Lamoureux and wife Hannah Clements he lost his way and had to stop to ask directions. The fellow he asked turned out to be a man named (you guessed it!) David Martin, who just happened to be an English teacher at the local high school.

Paul I. Edic, a genealogist of Akron, Ohio, was looking through a  Cleveland, Ohio telephone directory, scanning the name "Greenwood." He paused at what was apparently a misprint: "Encoh," for Enoch, Greenwood. For no especially good reason, he glanced at the complete listing for the name, and was mildly surprised to see the name of a street (Tarkington) that he recognized in the city. He also was somewhat startled to see that  Greenwood's house number on the street seemed to be familiar. As luck would have it, he happened to have his genealogical notes in a tablet lying nearby. It was true: the address, 16405 Tarkington Avenue, residence of Encoh/Enoch Greenwood in 1980 - was also the very same address of his grandparents, John and Agnes Hochewar, the year Paul Edic was born. As Paul remarks,

> "I felt sort of 'freaked out' and bemused over this strange coincidence: what could be the 'significance' of this happening, if any? Nowadays, I am inclined to regard this as no more than an odd, but remarkable, occurrence. Though I wonder what far-out theory or theories might people of a more metaphysical frame of mind propose or concoct?"

Well, those who are open to such things might suggest that Paul's story was indeed a classic synchronistic event: an a-causal coincidence having meaning to the person who experienced it.

Paul's story reminds me of one my friend Maralyn A. Wellauer of Milwaukee, Wisconsin, once shared with me:

"More than one of my 17th century Swiss family problems has been solved by consulting the "Bevoelkerungsverzeichnisse", Population Registers of Lists, found mainly in the Cantons of Zuerich and Thurgau. It wasn't until many years after I discovered this source, I learned that, in 1634, it was my direct ancestor, Johann Jakob Breitinger, who decreed that these rolls be kept.
Thanks, J.J.!"

As I have noted earlier, Carl Jung's concept of the "collective unconscious" also has long intrigued me. He believed that certain human traits are found in every community. Many of the images, folk tales, and metaphors found in various societies around the world are really the same, although they are  somewhat filtered by each culture. These images, which Jung described as "archetypes," emerge from this collective unconscious, sort of a universal pool of symbolic information that has developed and evolved over time. The whole human race has inherited this knowledge and has access to it via "Memories, Dreams, and Reflections" (the title of Jung's autobiography). He proposed that sometimes these unconscious archetypes invade our consciousness, carrying strong emotions, and - perhaps due to the archetypes not being bound by time and space - facilitate the occurrence of synchronistic events. Jung felt that meaningful coincidences - not meaningless chance groupings - seemed to be based on an archetypal foundation.

Heavy stuff, but, according to all the letters received, an area that has interested many of my colleagues. Some genealogists are very open to Jung's concepts. Harry Hollingsworth of Inglewood, California, stops to wonder:

"Could facts known by one's ancestors be 'stored' in his descendants, to be 'awakened' later?"

And in response to my letter, Maurice R. Hitt, Jr. of Binghamton, New York observes:

"I too am a believer in the 'collective unconscious' that you speak of."

Other family historians are more cautious. One good

friend, a co-editor of a prominent genealogical journal, wrote:

"There may well be such a thing as intuition, but I hesitate to attribute it to 'Jungian subconscious.' We have all experienced 'random patterning,' and when we work extensively on one subject like genealogy, we are going to make connections that seem miraculous. The key is whether they can be repeated. If not, I'd attribute the leap to the sheer cussed awfulness - or wonder - of things."

One of our most skilled genealogists is Eugene A. Stratton of Manchester, New Hampshire, who specializes in colonial New England and medieval English research. Gene looks at the subject at hand in relationship to one of his favorite subjects, genetics - about which he has written extensively in his well-reviewed book *Applied Genealogy*:

"The prevailing view among the experts on 'nature or nurture' seems to be that, yes, we are formed and guided through life by our genes, but, no, genes don't absorb our experience and pass it on. Given a set of genes, one generation might have changes in characteristics by mutation, but most mutations die with the individual. Those few changed genes that pass to more than one generation are changed not by the environment, but by accident, frequently in the process of chiasma, or crossing over.

The concept of chiasma in itself is fascinating. You may have lost all the genes from your great (seven times) grandfather, but still be carrying on the genes of Charlemagne. However, all I really want to point out here is that the learned experts seem to be against the possibility of genes 'learning.' Frankly, I don't want to believe the experts in this matter, but I can hardly ignore them. It is romantic to me to think that I'm not just carrying on the genes of my American ancestors, all of whom arrived in New England in the seventeenth century, as they received them from their English forebears, but that each generation may have added something to them. That is, that my New England ancestry was not just a mere conduit to pass along the inherited English characteristics, but that I am as well a New England-formed man as an England-formed man.

On the experts, I'm also impressed by how frequently today's solidly held scientific fact is tomorrow's obsolete fantasy. But, and I guess this is the important thing, as one who tends to worship evidence, I can point to no real evidence at all for my wishful thinking, so cannot recommend it to others."[1]

**Pastor David Jay Webber of Harwich, Massachusetts, states:**

"I know of Jung's 'collective unconscious' theory regarding the nature of intuition, yet I usually am more convinced that the perceptions of an individual's own subconscious mind serve as a credible explanation for many 'intuitive' phenomena. For example, my theory would hold that when someone is engaged in genealogical research, his subconscious mind registers all the data on a page of information from which his conscious mind is gleaning only one or two entries. The subconscious mind then derives clues from that subconsciously-perceived data which later impress themselves upon the conscious mind.

This theory may not account for all unexpected genealogical finds, but I think it would account for many of them. In summary, I think that in the course of their own research people often pick up clues as to where to do additional searching for a 'missing link,' yet at the time

---

[1]Gene is intrigued by some of the uncanny events that have happened in his personal life. He and his lovely wife Ginger have a belief that they were made for each other. He writes, "We got married in spite of considerable odds against it, impelled to a course of action over which we had no control. And we have the ability to read each other's minds, not infallibly, but more than enough to be coincidental. For example, my wife had a birthday while we were living in San Francisco. What to get her as a present? I went to Gump's, but could find nothing I wanted until I saw a pair of ivory Chinese chopsticks, which I bought. I went home and said to my wife, 'Guess what I got you for your birthday?' and she asked, 'A pair of ivory chopsticks?'"

they do not realize that they are picking up these clues."

William V. H. Barker of Shelton, Connecticut, agrees with Pastor Webber's view:

"I would give great weight in explaining unexpected genealogical discoveries to the activities of the *individual* subconscious, rather than the more esoteric *collective* subconscious. I believe that the subconscious mind active in each of us works over problems in a 'background' mode, while our conscious mind is otherwise directed. On the other hand, I do not wish to be styled as a logical conformist, and I recognize that if one always follows the most likely option one may well miss the opportunity to identify those strange and rare aspects that nature has permitted to exist."

One open to those rare aspects is Brenda Dougall Merriman of Guelph, Canada, who reflects:

"I was excited to receive your letter for two reasons! First, because at this time in my life, I am learning a little about the (scary but exciting) concept of a whole reality beyond our human and finite measurements of reality. Some people call this 'collective unconscious' or 'race memory' (or many other terms that I, as a fledgling metaphysician, still do not know). The 'significant other' in my life is a philosopher cum scientist who has spent years exploring this whole idea of how we humans are scarcely in touch with a real world of consciousness outside what we can sense, measure, and conceptualize within our own experience. I believe, and he believes, that occasionally we 'get in touch with' this bigger framework (whether through extra-sensory perception, meditation, or 'hunches,' or whatever name we call it) by sheer accident or by working hard at it.

So when I received your letter, I couldn't help getting this weird feeling that it happened to me again - something important in my life was getting validated and confirmed from a colleague in my favorite job. The second reason is more familiar - because I have had 'good luck' in finding missing ancestors or clues many times and identified with the happiness you expressed at making unexpected finds."

My genealogical colleague Professor Mark L. Wahlqvist of Melbourne, Australia, says:

"There is a theoretical possibility that factors operative between human beings might make the establishment of linkages, historical or contemporary, more likely. Human beings are, after all, not simply individuals, but family or societal creatures. I guess that, as a medical researcher, I am always looking for explanations as to why we make the observations we do, but I can imagine that there is some kind of 'collective intelligence' which allows us to proceed more successfully, many times, than we might expect. It does seem, as well, that 'chaos' or 'breakthrough' theory is very much on the side of genealogical research."

Family historian Dr. W. Cary Anderson of Decatur, Arkansas, remembers:

"I had sufficient experiences of 'allowing myself to be led' and following hunches in my genealogical quests to be able to use them in my written comprehensive exam for my Ed.D. degree in 1974. I was attempting to explain Jerome Bruner's *Structure of Knowledge*, and one member of my Committee, a professor of history, really took me to task on this - the only problem I had with my orals. I can still remember a couple of the other profs trying to stifle their laughter at how red-faced and sputtering he became trying to defend his narrow approach to the subject. But the Chairman of my Committee later told me it was as close as he had ever heard in explaining what Bruner meant. What I did was to combine Carl Jung's concepts with our intellectual training in a given field, and show how the two could work together to reach our answers!"

FOOD FOR THOUGHT, INDEED!

# 9
## *IT'S ALL IN THE TIMING*

"It's all in the timing." How often have we heard that overused phrase? And yet, according to my genealogical colleagues around the world, amazing coincidences - yes, synchronicities! - relating to the timing of certain "finds" are far from uncommon. They occur quite frequently and often help in propelling research forward towards successful results. Gerald J. Parsons of Syracuse, New York, remembers a strange event that happened in his youth:

"I got interested in family history in 1936 at the age of 11, and in 1939 I was put in touch with the late W. Herbert Wood, F.A.S.G., of New Haven, Connecticut. He was a distant relative and, like me, was interested in discovering the ancestry of Sarah, wife of my great-great-great grandfather Ephraim Gorham of Canterbury, Connecticut, and later Elbridge, New York. Nobody knew Sarah's maiden name, something that Herbert Wood had tried to find for many years before I even knew him. During the summer of 1939 while recuperating from having my tonsils removed, I received much family data from Herbert which I went over in great detail. On the afternoon of 7 August 1939, I intensively studied the Gorham material that Herbert had sent, and I said to myself 'I bet Sarah, wife of Ephraim Gorham, was a Staples!'

The very next day I received a letter from Herbert dated 7 August 1939 from New Haven which said in part, 'Today I had to go to the State Library at Hartford. While there, I had time to explore the ancestry of Sarah, wife of Ephraim Gorham. I called for the Probate papers of the estate of Jacob Staples of Canterbury, and, in the 1807 distribution of property to his widow Eunice Staples, I found mention of their second daughter, noted as Sarah, wife of Ephraim Gorham.'

I was stunned and thrilled at this discovery after all the years I had searched for her. At about the time the thought went through my mind that Sarah Gorham was a Staples, Herbert Wood was at the Connecticut State Library finding that she was indeed Sarah Staples! I wish I could have and have had more such experiences, but nothing ever so dramatic has happened to me since."

**Christine Rose, head of the thriving Rose Family Association, writes:**

"For many years I have experienced a phenomenon that I am totally unable to explain. I will get a letter from one part of the country with Rose family information. The writer may not even be a member of that particular Rose family, but happened upon the data. Then, within a day or two, (sometimes even on the same day!), I will get a letter or a phone call from another part of the country requesting information on that very same Rose group.

Then I've had instances where I haven't worked on a particular Rose family for two or three years, and then suddenly within days I'll receive several letters from people looking for that same Rose who don't even know each other. Or, sometimes when I haven't worked on a particular Rose family for years, within days of starting the new work, I will 'accidentally' run into material on the family in a totally unrelated file! This happens *often*. This type of coincidence used to unsettle me, but now I take it as a common, everyday occurrence. If you knew the huge number of early Roses, many unrelated, this phenomenon is even more amazing!"

**Dyan Kaye Sparling of Joshua Tree, California, can identify with what Christine Rose relates:**

"My overall Sparling family files currently consist of individual family group sheets for 1,719 Sparlings and 1,696 individual allied families, which equates to ca. 10,000 family members in file. I make mention of this because it shows what the odds would be in uniting two lost family members.

In the late 1970s Robert John Sparling was corresponding with me, and we were putting together his Colorado kin; *at exactly the same time,* Clarence Lester Sparling got in touch with me, and we were collecting data on his Irish ancestors. There was a one hundred year time difference between the two separate families. Clarence had an Irish ancestor shown on an early chart by the name of 'Benner Sparling,' and Robert John had an ancestor he knew nothing about named 'John B. Sparling.' None of us knew of any kind of a relationship between the two groups, but I had a very strong feeling that John B. and Benner were one and the same.

Following my hunch, I put the two families in touch with one another. The results were that they were not only first cousins, but also that they lived within six miles of each other! Clarence Lester Sparling passed away in December of 1991, but at least he had the happiness of getting to know his new close kin in the last years of his life that he would not otherwise have had."

We genealogists are not alone in having these experiences. F. David Peat in his profound *Synchronicity: The Bridge Between Matter and Mind* reenforces our perceptions of these occurrences by showing that sometimes certain synchronistic finds can indeed occur "inwardly" between different people. In discussing this phenomenon, he notes that historically there have been many occasions of important simultaneous discoveries made by scientists who are not in direct communication with each other. Some scientists often speak of ideas being "in the air," almost as if new concepts take the form of radio transmissions, complete in themselves but waiting for a competent receiver to pick them up. In 1858, for example, both Charles Darwin and Alfred Wallace came up with the theory of evolution, and even earlier there was the independent discovery of calculus by both Newton and Leibnitz.

When I was gathering material on Hunterdon County, New Jersey Germans for a section of my book *More Palatine Families*, Fred Sisser III was of great help to me. He had a marvelous talent for finding long-buried documents on this group, and his contributions to my final volume were immeasurable. We certainly were on the same wave-length as we pursued these Hunterdon families and often talked for hours long distance on the telephone coordinating our searches. The uncanny thing about our unplanned phone conversations was that eventually we both "knew" when the other would be calling! It got so strange that many times I would call Fred in New Jersey from my home in California, and he would pick up the phone and say "Hello, Hank" before I had even spoken a word. No matter what the hour, this occurrence happened over and over again!

Elissa Scalise Powell of Wexford, Pennsylvania, comments:

"I have always believed in those unbelievably magic moments when things seem to fall into place without any control from you. It has happened so much in my genealogical research that I almost start counting on some information appearing out of the blue *just at the time* I need it most!

Take today, for instance. My three year old got me up two hours earlier than normal, so what to do? I had some information on my husband's Bowman line sitting on my desk for at least three months, so I decided to enter it into my computer. I wrote a letter to one of the suppliers of the information asking for the title page and the preceding pages of ones she had sent me. I then called a member of my local genealogy club since she had mentioned having a part of a Bowman tree in one of her family histories. I decided to go look at the book myself, since she lived only ten minutes away. I would mail the letter I wrote along the way.

My friend's book turned out to be the *very same* one that I was writing away for more copies. It was a 41-page manuscript written 32 years ago. Thank goodness I hadn't mailed the letter yet! I had also thought to write to the other supplier of the information that had been sitting on my desk and prompt him for some promised reprinted photos. Voila! Upon arriving home, my mailbox had the pictures of our common ancestors going back to 1880!"

William W. Berkman gives yet another example of some pretty weird timing:

"Several years ago, I learned that a second great uncle, William M. Berkman, had a been a civil war veteran. I wrote to the National Archives, anticipating a delay of several months before I would receive a response. In the intervening period, I learned of a woman in Scipio, Indiana who was a third cousin and in possession of much family data. I corresponded with her frequently, and we exchanged material. Subsequently, I learned that she had received a copy of the data that I had requested (addressed to me) along with the information that she had requested on William M. Berkman. Each of us had requested the civil war information on William M. Berkman *on the very same day,* and we had not known of each other at the time!"

Carl Boyer, 3rd of Santa Clarita, California, has a good story to tell along these lines:

"My weirdest experience was when I wrote a letter to a mortuary asking if they might have the files of an older mortuary no longer in business. The State of New Jersey had no death certificate on file for my great-grandfather Jonathan Price Campbell, and I thought this might be a way to circumvent the problem. The lady wrote back promptly, saying she didn't have the records, but that she decided to take my letter to the local historical society meeting the night she received it.

She mentioned it to the first person she saw as she entered the door, asking 'Have you heard of a Jonathan Price Campbell?' The woman, who was looking at an old scrapbook, replied, 'Why yes, I'm reading his obituary at this moment!' The lady, Emma Huber, sent me a copy of the obituary and eventually of the death certificate, which finally turned up upon her request."

David Putnam, Jr., Correspondence Specialist at the Family History Library in Salt Lake City, shared a story recently:

"Neil Adair Putnam visited the Family History Library several times. He knew very little about his Putnam ancestry, but did bring with him a copy of his Putnam Family Bible. It had faded entries, but we were able to make out the names 'Benjamin' and 'Mary' on the parents' side of the family record. Neil had never heard those names before, and only knew of his descent from a Wilson Putnam of Henry County, Missouri, born about 1850. Subsequent research in various census rolls at the Library revealed that his Wilson was indeed son of Benjamin and Mary, but this was as far back as we could go. We were stymied.

Two days after Neil went back to Colorado, I remembered that I had just received a large box of materials from William Putnam, Jr. of Hyannis Port, Massachusetts. I recalled he was compiling the Putnam family lines of the Southern states. I opened the box, looked at the chapter on the Missouri families, and saw a section that made my heart skip: 'Benjamin Putnam of Henry County.' Within one half hour, I had the documented lineage of Wilson Putnam back to 1288 and John de Puttenham II of England. I am sure Neil Adair Putnam, at age 83, is delighted to have great tales of his forebears to tell his nine children. It just seems that Wilson and Benjamin Putnam wanted to be found that day and wanted to introduce themselves and their stalwart ancestors to Neil and his family!"

Rick Kampf of Vernon, British Columbia has a tale to tell where timing played a crucial role:

"My grandfather was a 'black sheep' who lost contact with his family shortly after he married my grandmother. He disappeared from my mother's life when she was twelve. My mother, with her younger sister and brother, then lived with various aunts and in foster homes while my grandmother worked as a housekeeper all around Saskatchewan.

When my grandmother died in 1970, my mother, Aldia Juelfs Kampf, found an address for an uncle in St. Paul, Minnesota of whose existence she had been only vaguely aware. She wrote this uncle to advise him of his sister-in-law's death, but he never responded.

Approximately ten to twelve years later, his daughter, Hazel Juelfs Kemper, was clearing out his effects shortly after his own death and found my mother's letter. She had no idea that she had had an uncle, much less a surviving cousin. So she immediately wrote to my mother.

In the interim, however , the home of my parents had been demolished. Time passed, and a mall was built on the site. The same street number of our house was now a shoe cobbler's shop. The mailman brought the letter in anyway and asked if the cobbler knew the people on the address. By coincidence, at that very time, my dad happened to have a pair of shoes in the shop being repaired. Seeing this, the mailman and the shoe repairman decided to stuff the letter into one of the shoes.

This all happened in the fall. My parents were 'snowbirds' at that time, so they took off for Indio, California for the winter and forgot all about the items they had left. About May of the following year, my dad finally remembered the shoes he had brought in for repair. Even though he thought they probably had been sold by then, he went back to the store to try and retrieve them. As luck would have it, there they were! When he brought the shoes home, he looked inside, found the letter, and gave it to my mother.

She wrote, Hazel phoned; they came out here, my folks went back there; my parents' oldest grandddaughter has become friends with Hazel's oldest daughter; I have visited several times and have a 'tee time' with Hazel's husband for late May this year. This has been a particularly wonderful experience for both ladies. I believe it has brought my mother's life to a full circle and filled a gap in her soul."

On October 8, 1984, Annette Kunselman Burgert of Myerstown, Pennsylvania, my co-author of *Westerwald To America*, had a birthday she'll never forget. Although successful at finding the ancestral German homes of many 18th-century immigrants to Pennsylvania, Annette had had no luck in documenting the European origins of her own Palatine ancestor, Bartholomai Kuntzelmann. On that special day, she was working alongside our mutual friend and Palatine researcher Carla Mittelstaedt-Kubaseck at the Heimatstelle Pfalz (now Institut für pfälzische Geschichte und Volkskunde) at Kaiserslautern, Germany.

Her research was interrupted when Carla leaned over and gave her a small scrap of paper, saying, "I know your maiden name was Kunselman. I found this notation in a churchbook I happened to be going through and thought it might be of interest to you." Annette's jaw fell open: the old entry Carla gave her from the Wendelsheim Lutheran Churchbook was the 1737 marriage record of her long-sought-for immigrant forebear, Bartholomai Kuntzelmann. That wonderful piece of information - found by chance - was the key to unlocking much of her entire German ancestry. What a present! Happy Birthday, Annette!

Judge John D. Austin writes:

"Two of my ancestors are Jesse Barker Sr. and Jr., father and son, both of whom served in the Revolution, the father dying in battle. That was about all I knew until 1957 when the late Edwin Neff of Tulsa, Oklahoma, discovered Connecticut land records proving a Brewster mother for Jesse Sr. and, accordingly, a *Mayflower* line. Thereupon, I undertook a project to identify all the descendants of Jesse Barker, Jr. of Edinburg, Saratoga County, New York. Jesse Jr. was the father of six children, all of whom married and left descendants. While I was generally successful in tracking the various families up to the present, I was stumped when it came to a single grandson, David Newton Barker. After a couple of years of digging, I set the notes aside.

In 1988, I attended a genealogical conference in Boston, but skipped the lectures one morning to enjoy a bit of research in the NEHGS Library. While seated in the Reading Room, I overheard a man at the next table mention to his companion words to the effect: 'I'm stuck on a father and son from Saratoga County, New York, who served in the Revolution. The father died in the War.'

I perked up my ears and hesitantly queried, 'Barker? From Edinburg?' I then introduced myself to retired Army General Rogers B. Finch of Little Silver, New Jersey. The unexpected encounter resulted in correspondence between us that gave him his Barker ancestry and a couple of *Mayflower* lines, and that gave me a real, live descendant of the mysterious David Newton Barker and complete records as to that lost branch!"

All kinds of strange events seem to happen to Helen L.

Harriss. She gave a recent talk to the Western Pennsylvania Genealogical Society on Pittsburgh's relationship to its rivers, especially the Ohio:

"After the talk, a member asked if I knew the location of a cave known as 'Smith's Cave,' which had Indian-era hieroglyphics. I had never heard of it - supposedly it was somewhere along the banks of the Ohio. Within five minutes of that conversation, another woman, a visitor from East Liverpool, Ohio, came up to talk to me. She asked a question concerning a story I had told of a pioneer family. She knew a similar story, an incident that had happened along the Ohio at - would you believe it - Smith's Cave, the one with the hieroglyphics. I can't remember when I've had such a quick answer to a question!"

Helen goes on to add:

"And just a few weeks ago, I was typing the draft for my Ohio River talk, and I was in the middle of a sentence about 'The Hill that Burns' (the Indian name for a hill along the Monongahela River which has a strata of coal near the surface). In fact, I was typing the words 'The Hill that Burns' when my phone rang. It was a client who was writing a book about some pioneer settlers, and his question was, ' Do you know where there is a hill known as 'The Hill that Burns?'"

Like so many others, Helen also marvels at the timing of certain finds:

"Not only do weird things happen to me in my own research - they also occur when I'm working for others. I've had so many instances when someone has hired me to work on a family with which I am already familiar. I am continually matching a client with another working on the same line; of the various professional researchers in this area, they could have as easily chosen someone who did not know the particular family. As the result of one such experience, a family society was formed among the ones who hired me, and they made me an honorary member!"

Hudson Valley genealogist Barbara Smith Buys tells of often finding exactly what she's looking for in an unexpected place and how timing can play a crucial part in searching:

"One day in 1980, I was doing research for a client in

Albany. I was not sure whether to go to check surrogate's and county clerk's records that day or to go to the New York State Library. Something told me (and I'm sure it was God's guidance) to go to the Surrogate's Office.

After being there for about ten minutes, a gentleman came into the room, and we passed the time talking. He asked me what I was doing, and I told him that I was working on the Litchfield family which lived in the town of Coeymans. He asked, 'Leonard Litchfield?' I replied, 'the same.' It turned out that he and his wife lived on the Litchfield property and had been interested enough to copy the old gravestones in the family plot there some years before. They sent me the whole record of that cemetery, together with a notarized statement (he was an attorney) attesting to its accuracy and authenticity.

How can anyone be that lucky?! I have always felt that I live under a lucky star and am most grateful for a wonderful life with marvelous experiences such as this one!"

Sometimes it helps to be working at the genealogical library on the same day and time as someone else. Nell Sachse Woodard of Oceanside, California, observes:

"My philosophy about genealogy is simply this: there is no such thing as coincidence when seeking ancestors, mine or someone else's. When the time arrives that you are truly ready for the information which you are seeking, you will have it. And beating your brains out to find a particular bit of information is useless. My feeling is that you do all of the things that you would do in locating the data and then stop pushing. That item will be on hand in its own good time.

Perhaps this incident will illustrate: a student of mine was interested in a South Carolina lineage. While she was taking my class in genealogy, she and her sister went to that state to pursue some research. When they arrived, they found a rhododendron festival was in full swing and that housing was at a minimum. While they were at the airport, they 'ran into' a rather genteel lady who took them under their wing and offered them a room in her home. She fed them and saw them safely to the library where they were to spend the day. Since every native was out doing the gala event, the library was deserted. Only one librarian, some staff members, and the two sisters were present.

Sometime during the day, a prim, prissy, little elderly man came in and inquired of the librarian for the location of a book. She was going to assist him, but he pointedly told her that just the location would be sufficient. He chose two books and brought them to the only table that was then occupied, the two sister's working place. When the ladies realized that the information they were seeking was not where they had hoped it would be, the two decided to call it a day and return later. But the two books, abandoned by the little man when he had finished with them, were still on the table where he had left them.

The sister asked if they should put the books back on the proper shelf, and she was told that perhaps they should do so. Each took one, and both idly started looking through their respective indexes. To their utter amazement, the references that they were seeking were in the two books!

Coincidence? Never!!!"

That elderly man who leaves books on tables down in South Carolina seems to have gone north. Ask Faith G. Haungs of Lockport, New York:

"Five years ago, I hired a German genealogist to find the precise origins for my Haungs family of Baden. After many months, I received a short letter from him stating that he had found nothing. Then, six months ago, he wrote again and told me he had unexpectedly found my Haungs ancestors while doing research for another client. He traced my line back to a Dionis Haungs, born in 1785, in Moos, Baden.

The following week I was in the Erie County Library researching another family line. An elderly man sat down at my table and, for two hours, read a German phone book. When he departed, he rudely left the phone book on the table, instead of returning it to where it belonged. As I was leaving, I was going to return my books to the proper shelves and decided to pick up the phone book too. As I bent to lift the book, I noticed the name 'Haungs' pop out at me. I quickly sat down and started to read. To my disbelief, there was a Dionis Haungs living in Baden-Baden, which is only a short distance from Moos.

The very next day I wrote to this Dionis Haungs, hoping that with the name 'Dionis' he might know more about my Haungs family, or at least know of someone who did. I recently received his reply. Our ancestors were *brothers* in Moos. He had been researching the same family for years. He told me about our forebears, the history of Moos, and also about the Catholic Church there called 'St. Dionis.' (Strangely enough, St. Dionis Feast Day is on October 9th - the date of my wedding anniversary). So from one letter, to an address I accidentally found in a phone book, I discovered a new relative, the history of my ancestral home, and - best of all - three more generations of Haungs going back thirteen generations into the 1600's!"

**Dewayne E. Perry of Summit, New Jersey, also had a memorable incident involving timing at a library:**

"I was searching for data on Fanny Polley, who married at Lisbon, Connecticut 5 November 1851 to my wife's great-grandfather John William Mell. The only other information I could find at the time was a record of a Fanny Polly, aged 16 and born in Connecticut, listed in the 1850 census of Lisbon living with a Bramin family. Her age seemed correct, but our family had a tradition that she was from Pennsylvania and had some sort of a Mather connection. Subsequent searches always ended in frustration, with no ties documented between the Pollys and my wife's Fanny Polley.

However, one day when my wife and I were working at the Connecticut State Library, I had an incredible piece of good luck! As I walked by a file cabinet with an open drawer, a folder with the name Polley caught my eye. Inside was a copy of the family Bible record of Johnson Fitch Polley and his wife Kesiah *Mather* Rodgers. There on the list of their children was Fanny Polley, born 25 July 1833 in Milford, *Pennsylvania* who married John William Mell. Eureka! That happenstance was the key to unlocking a whole new set of ancestors."

Carol Willsey Bell recently received a call from a man in Tennessee who was investigating General Emerson Opdycke, who had commanded an Ohio regiment during the civil war at the Battle of Franklin. He was hoping she could add some genealogical background to what was known about the soldier militarily. Carol had two thick files of data to help him which elated the gentleman no end. While the call was going on, she says:

"One of my regular patrons in the library, Mr. Moore, was quietly working. As soon as I hung up, Mr. Moore mentioned that his own great grandfather had served under Opdycke and had participated in the Battle of Franklin. Further, he even had his ancestor's diary relating to the occurrences of that day! As he went on about the battle, he happened to mention that General Cox was also in that fight. I interrupted him and said, 'Our General Cox?' His answer was, 'Yes, General Jacob Cox from Warren, Ohio.' So, as a result of that conversation, I can now also send information on Cox to the man in Tennessee, as well as some of the treasures from Mr. Moore's personal collections relating to his ancestor's participation in the battle. Was it pure luck as to the timing of all this, or something else???"

After I spoke at the Palatines To America Conference in Adrian, Michigan in 1984, a clergyman, Reverend Shuster, came up and told me a wonderful story. For years he had wished to visit the hometown of one of his ancestors in another state and especially had hoped to be able to find his forefather's tombstone in the old graveyard there. After years of being unable to visit the area due to ministerial duties, he finally was able to put work aside and make his long-awaited trip.

He arrived at the town and went directly to its old, rather large cemetery. Reverend Shuster sought out the sexton and asked him if he happened to know the location of his ancestor's stone. To his surprise, the sexton led him immediately to the grave.

Reverend Shuster expressed his amazement that the sexton knew the precise whereabouts of the grave without having to go back to the office and look up its location in the files. The sexton remarked that Reverend Shuster was the *fifth* person that day to inquire about the stone. He then pointed to a hollow on the hill overlooking the cemetery where the Shuster Family Reunion was taking place.

The minister had known absolutely nothing of this event prior to his visit. He rushed over to the hillside gathering and was able to meet and greet many of his long-lost relatives!

TALK ABOUT TIMING!

## *1 0*
## *SMALL WORLD, ISN'T IT?*

The late, beloved John Insley Coddington, one of the founding Fellows of the American Society of Genealogists, loved to regale younger family historians with his marvelous stories culled from many years in the field. Rabbi Malcolm H. Stern kindly supplied me with a tape of a banquet speech given by John to the National Genealogical Society in 1981. As usual on this occasion, John was in his inimitable fine form, the king of genealogical raconteurs.

One long and lively anecdote involved a piece he had written for the *National Genealogical Society Quarterly* on one John Taylor of Milford, Delaware. The article found its way to the desk of Dr. Jean Stephenson who was then the verifying genealogist of the D.A.R. The very next day after she had read the article, Dr. Stephenson received a letter from a lady named Phyllis in Crockett, Texas, asking about the very same John Taylor. The lady mentioned that years ago she had seen an old family Bible in which all the Taylors were recorded. The Bible was once with a cousin in Elkhart, Indiana, but Phyllis didn't know its present whereabouts as her relative remarried to a man whose name she didn't know and moved to a place nearby with a funny name (which she couldn't recall).

Ever-the-indefatigable searcher, John went to Elkhart to try and track down the book. As luck would have it, Coddington had a former student, now a lawyer, who lived there. He told his old friend, "I'm looking for the cousin of a lady named Phyllis in Crockett, Texas who is named 'Something-or-other.' She used to live in Elkhart, and then she married somebody else and moved to a town with a funny name." The lawyer said, "I know who you mean! I handled her divorce from her first husband, and the town with the funny name you're looking for is 'Mishawaka.'" John then went on and on with his memorable banquet talk, milking this genealogical-shaggy-dog-story for all it was worth. After many more crooks and turns, the tale finally reached its happy ending, as John went to Mishawaka, found the cousin, located the Bible, and extracted pages of long-sought-for Taylor family names and dates!

It was indeed a remarkable chain of "who-do-you-know" coincidences (mixed in with some good timing) that eventually led John Insley Coddington to find that old family Bible. But perhaps such events are not really all that surprising. John Allen Paulos in his *Beyond Numeracy* tells his readers that if two people sit next to each other on an airplane, chances are 99 out of 100 that there are fewer than two intermediates between them. An intermediate might be a professor who has taught you and the other person's sister, for example. Paulos makes this mathematical statement based on each person having 1,500 or so acquaintances. This thesis may hold true, judging from the volume of responses I have received detailing experiences along these lines.

Mary K. Meyer gives a great illustration of this phenomenon:

"I just happen to live within a few miles of the Family Line Publications Bookstore, and, as the owner is a friend, I often drop by to look over the new titles, catch up on the latest genealogical gossip, or pick a brain. One one such occasion, I was introduced to a new employee, a young man who had recently arrived in Maryland from Madison, Wisconsin. I exchanged polite conversation with Jim, and one thing led to another as conversations between genealogists will. I asked, 'Where are you from, and where were your ancestors from?' 'New York,' replied Jim. 'Really,' said I, 'and what county might they have been from?' 'Why, Washington County,' responded Jim.

'That so,' said I. 'I had ancestors there too. What were your ancestors' names?' 'Switzer,' replied Jim. 'They were with those Irish Germans who came over with Philip Embury.' 'Really,' said I, 'one of my ancestor's daughters married a man named Christopher Switzer.' Jim got excited and said, 'Christopher Switzer was brother to my ancestor!'

That should have concluded our great coincidental conversation, but there was more to come. 'What was the name of your ancestor's daughter who married Christopher Switzer?' asked Jim. 'Oh, her name was Orra Horton,' said I - 'but they disappear, and I could never trace them.'

'They went to Canada,' said Jim, and he continued, 'I know a woman who lives in Kingston, Ontario who has been looking for Christopher's wife's name for over twenty years!' Jim called her that night to give her the good news, and she followed up with a long letter. She and I have shared much information since then.

Coincidence? Serendipity? No, the Great God of Genealogy was at it again! Surely, it was his hand that guided Jim's wife to take a new job in Baltimore; that steered Jim to Family Line Publications in Westminster, Maryland; that motivated Jim and me to strike up our 'polite' conversation that day. But the strangest part of all is that Jim's wife didn't like her new job in Baltimore and, two months after our initial meeting, Jim, his wife, and two children returned back home to live in Madison, Wisconsin. Oh the Great God of Genealogy works in mysterious ways!"

Nick Vine Hall of Albert Park, Australia, loves to trace the sequence of events in coincidental occurrences and how they unfold. One such "chain" began several years ago when (1) Nick wrote an article in the *National Genealogical Society Quarterly* on "Americans Down Under" and happened to mention the Gougenheim sisters, Americans who came to Australia in the 1800s. (2) Francis James ("Jim") Dallett, F.A.S.G., of Taconic, Connecticut read the article and wrote to Nick about the Gougenheim sisters, whom he had done some work on for a genealogical article in the U.S.A. previously. (3) Nick wrote back to Jim, and, for some reason which he cannot fathom, mentioned his Huguenot ancestors from the village of Ruffec. (4) Jim answered and noted that HIS Huguenot forefathers also came from Ruffec. (5) Nick wrote back to Jim and inquired if he might stop by and visit him after attending the 1992 National Genealogical Society

Conference in Jacksonville. (6) Jim replied, "Of course." (7) Nick arrived in Connecticut, and was given a grand tour of New England by the hospitable Jim and Charlotte Dallett. (8) So that Nick could meet other eminent genealogists, Jim decided to invite C. Frederick Kaufholz, F.A.S.G., who just happened to live nearby, to breakfast. (9) In casual conversation between the Wheaties and scrambled eggs, Nick offhandedly remarked to Fred Kaufholz that he had a client, Professor Mark Wahlqvist of Australia, who had German ancestry leading back to a place called Duderstadt. (10) Fred, completely unknown to Nick, was famous for being the world's leading expert on the town of Duderstadt and asked what family Professor Wahlqvist descended from? (11) Nick replied, "the Kaesehagen family," whereupon (12) Fred Kaufholz then produced right off the top of his head about six generations of the good Professor's ancestry back to about 1650. This long-shot connection all came about, notes Nick Vine Hall, because two American ladies, who were no relation to the Professor or to any of the rest of the people involved, just happened to come to Australia in the last century.

Nick has many similar stories to tell. One concerns the return of two old Case family albums to him in 1985. These old photo books dated back to Wiltshire, England in the 1870s, and, unfortunately, were sold off by the executors of his Hungarian step-grandmother's estate in a Salvation Army sale in the 1960s. The stranger who bought them purchased them, she said, because she "fell in love with the dashing young man in the front picture" (Nick's grandfather in 1899). As Nick remembers:

"This all happened in Sydney, a city of some three million people. In the 1980's, I was Director of the Society of Australian Genealogists in Sydney, and had made up a family tree of faces to inspire the Society's 8,000 members to explore family photographs. This tree was on display in the Australian Reading Room of our organization. A lady who was in the library one day happened to recognize a picture of my mother in her youth on the big pictorial family tree exhibit. That same picture was in the missing albums - the ones she had purchased at the sale years before. So this DEAR lady, Mrs. Loretta Shackley, came to the reception area and said to my secretary, 'Would you please ask the Director if his family is a few albums short?"

GeLee Corley Hendrix of Greenville, South Carolina, talks about meeting the right person at the right time, and the "spooky feelings" brought on sometimes when a record finally turns up that ties up loose ends of years of research:

"There have been several such findings. I attended the annual meeting of the Orangeburgh German Swiss Genealogical Society one year. One of the events was a tour given by Hugo Ackerman, curator of the A. S. Salley Library housed by the Orangeburgh Historical Society. Through a casual conversation with him, I bemoaned my hang-up on the Bond family of Orangeburgh District. He left me briefly to return with a folder containing the original deeds pertaining to John Bond. Bond's signature on the deed solved my problem. The puzzle pieces of years of research then fell into place with enough documentation to back my evaluation of the family structure, and I published my study in the December 1991 *National Genealogical Society Quarterly.* I, in turn, later received an enthusiastic call from a minister in Pennsylvania who had seen my Bond article stating that 'he was led' to it as a means to answer his own genealogical problem through me and my research."

Dr. John Terence Golden of Columbus, Ohio, had an interesting experience a few years back:

"In my own research, I tend to play hunches and also seem to have good luck. Starting in 1972, I began my genealogical research with a 'Blitzkrieg' in which I gathered information from all older relatives, wrote up the family history as best I could, and then sent copies to all my relatives hoping for more from them in return. I began to make good progress, but my Irish lines were more difficult than the others, due to the scarcity of written records there. I did learn that my Irish Moran family came from near Tuam in County Galway and made initial efforts to obtain more data on that line.

But an unusual stroke of luck really broke things open, enabling me to make a firmer connection with my Irish relatives. One of my older relatives who had been given a copy of my Moran family history and genealogy decided to do some remodeling. She was a granddaughter of the immigrant Thomas Moran and lived in the house he had built. In tearing out a wall, there fell from behind a fireplace a letter dated 'Toaher Luneth 19, 1885.' It was to my Thomas Moran from a brother Tim in Ireland and told of several other relatives and their whereabouts.

I then sent a letter to the Postmaster in Tuam and, on a hunch, enclosed a genealogical chart of my family. He sent back a nice note and suggested that I contact a Mr. Dunleavy at Barbersfort near Tuam who was an older resident of the area interested in genealogy. I wrote Mr. Dunleavy and told him that I would be coming to Ireland soon and would like to meet him. He agreed, and we finally got together a few months later.

What a revelation that was! Patrick Dunleavy, it turned out, was a pleasant Irish gentleman in his 80's, the sole survivor of a family of fifteen children, who had fought in the rebellion and had been awarded five medals. He helped clear up the mysterious parts of that 1885 letter, 'Luneth' meant 'August,' and 'Toaher' (now 'Togher') was actually a townland that I had just walked across in Tuam.

Most remarkable of all, Mr. Dunleavy was a grandson of the Tim Moran who had written the letter to my immigrant ancestor Thomas in 1885! He had heard that a brother had gone to America or Australia, but had never known the details. He said that the Morans in Ireland had one trait in common: 'We all have a fondness for the drink.' I told him that was true of the American Morans also, and we had a toast of Irish whiskey to celebrate the reunion!"

**Donald R. Brown of Myerstown and Harrisburg, Pennsylvania makes an interesting observation:,**

"Frequently, when standing in cafeteria lines such as the ones in 1991's Palatines To America Conference at Cobleskill, New York, fate placed me alongside someone who needed information that I knew."

That sort of thing has happened many times to me also. For example, on a recent trip to Scandinavia, my wife Bonnie and I found ourselves seated across the dining table in Bergen, Norway, from a Dr. George E. Fissel of Pinehurst, North Carolina. We struck up a conversation that eventually led to a discussion of my work on the Palatines. For years, Dr. Fissel had longed to find more information on his heritage. He had even gone to Germany looking for anyone who bore his rather unusual surname, but had no luck in tracking his family down.

Somewhat timidly, he inquired if I'd ever heard the name. Not only did I know of his family and of their emigration in 1742, I even was able to tell him his ancestral town (Essenheim), as the Fissel/Fischel family figured prominently in two of my books *The Palatine Families of Ireland* and *More Palatine Families*. There were over 45 other individuals that particular evening half-way around the world with whom we could have been seated, but good old serendipity put us together!

Neil Morgan had a column dated January 6, 1992 in the *San Diego Tribune* that reported the story of Ken Blucher, former assistant police chief in that city. Mr. Blucher recently was on a motor-coach tour in Nova Scotia, where his grandfather had been born. By pure chance, he went to a local restaurant and asked the waitress if she knew any Morrisons, one of his family names. "That's *my* name," she replied. And when his bus rolled back through the town the next day, she brought names and burial sites for six of his grandfather's brothers and two sisters - all of them news to Mr. Blucher!

Anna Harvey of Richmond, Vermont, was looking for the brother of her grandmother Snyder, all the rest of her family being accounted for. Someone had told her that there were Snyders in Ticonderoga, New York and gave her the name of one of them. Mrs. Harvey didn't wait to write this individual; instead, she telephoned the town clerk directly to see if she knew of such a person. The clerk said, "Yes, she's my office assistant." The newly-found relative was then able to give Mrs. Harvey many details about her branch of the Snyder family.

Nancy Alcook Vannoller of Coopersville, Michigan, visited her aunt in Eau Claire, Michigan recently on the 4th of July. She recalls,

"The town had a nice parade which included a number of Civil War reenactors. That afternoon, my husband and I visited their camp, and I started to talk with one of the many soldiers. He made the remark that he had a Civil War ancestor, and I stated I did also. He said his ancestor enlisted in 1864 in February and died in July. This interested me because my ancestor also had died in July of that year. I asked where his forefather had enlisted, and he said Kalamazoo. More coincidence ... mine had also. He asked me what unit my ancestor was in, and I replied the 11th infantry. When he said that his was also in that unit, I knew they had to have been neighbors. I asked him what his ancestor's name was, and he said John Brown Alcook.

I'm sure my chin hit the ground. He had just named my grandfather. John was his great grandfather. But the story doesn't end here. His grandmother and my dad were brother and sister, but, because of their age difference, I had never met him and had only met his mother once many years before. Needless to say, my new found cousin, Milton Foster, and I had a very enjoyable afternoon trading information and addresses. It truly can be a small world!"

Family historian Franklin A. Zirkle of Roanoke, Virginia, relates:

"My wife Penny decided last January that she would replace the picture hanging above our fireplace mantel. It was about the same color as our wall covering, and she wanted one that contrasted better. She returned from an antique shop carrying a large unframed picture. She sat it on the mantel and asked me to look at it. I walked across the room and stood before the picture, a lovely snow scene of an old mill. I asked where the mill actually was located. Penny replied that the sales clerk had said it was in West Virginia. I looked closer and saw a name at the bottom that said, 'Forestville Mill.' I turned to her and said, 'that mill was built by *your* ancestors about 1750, who then sold it to *my* ancestors in 1757!'

We spent the next ten minutes picking up her teeth!"

Roger K. Rasmussen of Salem, Oregon, has quite a "It's A Small World" story to tell:

"My ninety-year-old great aunt, Agnes, gave me her treasury of family photographs a few months ago. Included was a very old picture of an Indian woman and four children; however, there were no names or other identification on it, so I called her about it.

My great-great grandmother, Catherine Amelia (Sage) Lansing, was hired as the housekeeper for a white man and his part Indian children after the death of his Indian wife. They lived on the Blackfeet Indian Reservation near the town of Browning, Montana. She lived there during the period of 1898 to about 1908. Agnes lived with them for part of this time. I neglected to ask for the name of the family assuming that she would not remember.

An acquaintance of mine, through my business, Mr. Stone, had mentioned that he was part Indian and from Montana, so I thought I would relate the story. He confirmed that indeed he was one-quarter Indian, and he was from the Blackfeet Reservation. I asked if he knew anyone there who might be able to identify anyone in the picture. He said that he knew many people there, and that he had an elderly uncle who was still alive who might be of some help. Mr. Stone asked if I had any names at all, and I replied that I didn't but could check with my aunt. I had copies made of the picture for him to send along with the skimpy bits of information that I had.

I contacted my Aunt Agnes, and she said that they had lived with a wonderful man named 'Mr. Stone.' I almost fell over! I called my friend and related what I had just learned. He in turn called his uncle in Montana and asked him if the family had ever had a housekeeper and, if so, what her name was. He said that after his mother had died his father had hired a housekeeper named 'Mrs. Lansing.' The children had wanted their father to marry her, but he had married someone else, and she had moved away.

Eighty years and almost a thousand miles away, the families cross paths again. I now had the names, a wonderful addition to the family history and a new 'uncle.'"

And then there are the strange occurrences that can happen at a genealogical lecture. I think that because a really top-notch lecturer always communicates in an interesting and positive way, good returns benefiting all parties present are inevitable. Time and time again we are shown the incredible amount of experiences and information we have in common. Veteran speakers, then, have learned to expect the unexpected after their talks. Dr. Raymond Martin  Bell of Washington, Pennsylvania, affirms,

> "An advantage to speaking to genealogical groups is that I nearly always gain something. At Silver Spring, Maryland, a woman was able to tell me where in Alsace my Ensminger ancestors originated. At Dodge City, Kansas, I was shown a history of my home county (Washington) that I had never seen. Later I got a copy."

During a session of the Tercentenary Conference of the Huguenot Society in London in 1987, Nick Vine Hall made a chance remark mentioning his ancestor John Roubel (c. 1744 -1825), a Huguenot silversmith of Somersetshire. A lady in the audience of 300 people came up to him at tea break, and said she just happened to remember seeing some old court dockets noting this rare surname in a bundle of papers in the Gloucestershire Record Office. She added that some of the bills for services rendered in the 1800 - 1808 period bore John Roubel's letterhead. All this wonderful material was not only in a different English county than the family's previously-known residence, but also had never been indexed in the catalogue of papers under the Roubel name at all! In all likelihood, Nick would never have found this information had not the woman been in attendance and had not he offhandedly mentioned his ancestor. The good lady fortunately knew the correct reference number for Nick to obtain this crucial bundle of documents, which then enabled him to extend his line far back in time.

A similar experience again happened to Nick at the Fourth Australasian Congress on Heraldry and Genealogy in Canberra in 1986:

> "I was a plenary session speaker and often mention my

own family studies as examples to make a point. Like a rabbit out of a hat, a man in the audience came up with a long lost branch of my family who, he informed me, had become tea planters in Ceylon in the 1870's. They 'just happened' to have married into HIS family. No wonder we couldn't find them in old England! Again, this coincidence came about through the mention of an unusual family name ('Buxton Forbes Laurie') in a public forum before a live audience of 600 genealogists."

Percy William ("Bill") Filby, prolific co-author of *Passenger & Immigration Lists Index, Who's Who in Genealogy & Heraldry*, and other helpful volumes, had a memorable experience at one of his talks:

"When I go to give a lecture, I select totally *at random* one edition of *Passenger & Immigration Lists Index* to illustrate to my listeners how my books can be used. Each volume contains about 250,000 names, but there were *millions* who came over to America across the centuries, so the chance of finding a particular name in any one volume is very, very small.

While we were waiting for the meeting to begin, the person who was to be my 'introducer' casually picked up the one volume I decided to show during my lecture. After a moment, she let out a scream! Her family had come from Russia, having been Germans who settled there. When the families started leaving Russia for Germany or America, I recorded what had been listed in the journals of Germans from Russia in my index. There were perhaps 5,000 such in this one volume, and there my introducer found all six of her family who had left Russia for Germany/U.S.A. She had spent many hours over ten years looking for this family, and here they all were with ages, occupations, places of origin in Russia, the ship upon which they came to the new world, and even where they settled in America."

Dr. Raymond M. Bell remembers several other instances where he experienced serendipitous encounters. One was when he was working in the Martinsburg, West Virginia Library on his Seibert family. As he was researching the family, by chance a young man walked in who turned out to be the son of the local Seibert historian. The data he possessed cleared up many puzzles that had stymied Professor Bell over the years.

On another occasion, he was investigating records at the Shelbyville, Kentucky courthouse. He asked the woman in charge where the early will books of the county were. She asked him just what family he was working on. It turned out that Professor Bell was looking up the lady's very own Fullenwider line, and he was able to share data with her that she was not aware of.

Another time, Professor Bell (who is also an amateur radio operator) was talking to a man in Ohio and happened to mention that he was a genealogist looking up the Trimmer ancestry of Richard Nixon. The man, a complete stranger, said he had a neighbor named Trimmer. Professor Bell contacted the neighbor and, as a result, got a copy of a rare 1904 family manuscript, previously unknown!

Then, on yet another investigation while looking for material on the Williamson family of Pennsylvania, Professor Bell got in touch with a woman in Iowa who was also seeking information on the family. Sometime later, he received a letter from her with a copy from a Florida genealogical magazine of a Williamson family history. He called the lady in Florida who had submitted it. The woman then mentioned that, while in a New Jersey courthouse, she remarked to a fellow researcher that she was looking up old families, one of which was named Williamson. Surprisingly, the second woman said that she had an old Williamson manuscript in her possession. As it was of little use to her, she gave it to the Florida lady. It had been found in a vacant house which the second lady's husband was remodeling. It turned out to be an accurate, hand-written account, over 100 years old, that tied together various branches of the Pennsylvania Williamson family. What a chain of people and events it took to finally get to a marvelous find!

Dexter Hawn of Ottawa, Ontario, was researching his maternal ancestor Jacob Schnäbelin/Schneebeli who had married in Germany in 1655. He had been born in Switzerland, but no details were known concerning his date or place of birth. Dexter felt that the chances of tracing

Schnäbelin in his native village or town seemed rather remote, especially in view of the early time period. He did learn, however, of the occurrence of the surname in 17th-century records of Affoltern am Albis in Canton Zürich. So, without much expectation of success, he wrote the central archives of that canton.

He was delighted when word came from there that the name "Jagli Schnewli" (the Swiss equivalent of "Jacob Schnäbelin"), son of Rudolf Schnewli, appeared in their emigration indexes for the relevant time period, and that the name of the village in Germany to which he had emigrated was also given (agreeing with data Dexter already had found). Eventually, he was able to trace Jacob (Jagli) Schnäbelin/Schnewli to his great-grandfather Heini Snewli, born ca. 1530 at Affoltern am Albis.

Dexter then decided to hire a researcher in Salt Lake City to check Swiss sources at the Family History Library which were not available in Canada on interlibrary loan. He was amazed when he received a letter dated 30 September 1985 from his Salt Lake genealogist mentioning that further research in the archives was unnecessary, because the work had been done by her already. It seems that Dexter's researcher, whom he had not known previously, also descended from the Schnäbelin/Schnewlis of Affoltern am Albis, and she had been gathering documented data on the family for years! As the researcher noted at the bottom of her letter to Dexter Hawn, "Small world, isn't it!!??"

Elizabeth Whitten of Huntsville, Alabama, was traveling through the east gathering data on her Moore family line. She had spent some successful hours at the Lancaster County, Pennsylvania Historical Society Library and had written her findings on a particular sheet of paper. However, as she continued her investigations, she realized that somehow the Moore material found at Lancaster had been misplaced. She looked and looked for the information, but to no avail. So she continued her trip, somewhat handicapped by the loss of the data.

The first day home, a call came from a lady in Pennsylvania. She said that she had found Mrs. Whitten's notes in the Lancaster County Historical Library and had asked the librarian about them. She replied that they had been there several days. The lady noted that the paper showed data on the Moore line, so she checked the guest registration, found Mrs. Whitten's address as one working on that family, and called her. Mrs. Whitten's happiness at the recovery of her materials was compounded when the woman who had found the paper told her that she also was a direct descendant of that very same Moore family. The woman generously shared her own family data and was able to tell Mrs. Whitten "all she needed to know" to complete her research on the line!

Frederick T. Newbraugh of Berkeley Springs, West Virginia, remembers when he was having a hard time tracking down land records regarding his ancestor Henry Hollingersworth of Pennsylvania and then Maryland. One day a gentleman visited him seeking help on a West Virginia surname, one of Fred's areas of expertise. When he was about to leave, on a pure wild impulse, Fred asked him if he might know something about Henry Hollingersworth The man surprisingly replied that, not only did he know about the family, but his very home was on a part of the original Hollingersworth family farm!

Helen L. Harriss recalls a case when she started work for a client, and, surprisingly, found that his ancestor had lived on her very street. She then asked an elderly lady who had resided in the area for all of her life if she had ever heard of the particular woman's name that they were seeking. Amazingly, it was the elderly lady's own mother's aunt. She was the "Aunt Mary" that Helen had often heard of in her youth, and Aunt Mary had even died in the elderly lady's home. Helen had used her lovely china and silver at parties, and all she had to do was go up into the elderly woman's attic to find the family records she was seeking. Had the client hired anyone else, he wouldn't have fallen heir to all he did!

Carol Willsey Bell of Ohio met Mary Keysor Meyer of Maryland when both were Genealogical Librarians at their respective state societies. They both had common ground in their employment, and even discovered within the first five minutes of their meeting that they had a common ancestral line, the Allings from New Haven, Connecticut.  Carol relates:

"On one of Mary's visits to Ohio, I had to continue to go to work, which was fine with her, because she came to work with me and worked in the library. One day while she was there, I was talking with a researcher who was interested in an early aviator from Trumbull County, about whom we had much data. Discussion got around to the famous Cleveland Air Races, and I mentioned that when my grandparents lived in Cleveland, their neighbor across the street was one Cook Clelland, very famous for his participation in the races. I played with his children whenever I visited. Mary overheard this discussion and came over and said, 'Cook Clelland was from my hometown, and I was born on his parents' farm in Greenwich, Huron County, Ohio!!!' Small World???"

I'LL SAY !

# 11
# DR. JOAN MITCHELL'S STORY

Sometimes several kinds of serendipitous experiences are encompassed in one story. Dr. Joan Kirchman Mitchell of Tuscaloosa, Alabama, has such a tale to tell - and it's a wonderful one! She calls it "The Serendipitous Journey To Find Johann Frederick Kirchmann:"

"I became interested in my family's history and genealogy in the 1970's but had very limited information about my paternal great grandfather John Kirchman (Johann Frederick Kirchmann) and his wife Mary Mayn Kirchman. I did know that their son Henry lived in White Sulpher Springs, Montana from the time he was ten or so (ca. 1880) until his early thirties (ca. 1905). I also knew that, at some point, John Kirchman had left his wife and their six children in White Sulpher Springs and never returned. The family story said that John went back to St. Louis where he had once resided, married again, and had another family.

SERENDIPITY #1 - THE ARTICLE THAT FELL INTO MY LAP:
In the fall of 1979, I was browsing in the periodical section of the University of Alabama Library and noticed on a top shelf, way over my head where I normally do not browse, the bright red covers of an incomplete set of the *Journal of the Montana Historical Society*. I stretched up as high as I could and randomly tipped one of the volumes from the shelf. In the process, I lost my balance and dropped to a semi-squatting position. The journal literally fell into my lap and opened to an article about the *Rocky Mountain Husbandman*, a weekly newspaper published in White Sulpher Springs from 1875 to 1904.

I sat there stunned for a few seconds. I couldn't believe my good fortune. The article led me to the Montana Historical Society in Helena, MT. I wrote and asked if they had the *Husbandman* on microfilm. They replied that they did and would loan two reels at a time through interlibrary loan. So I requested the first two reels. In the personal section of the third issue, 9 December 1875, I found the following information on Charles and Henry Mayn, brothers of Mary Mayn Kirchman:

> *'Mr. Henry Mayn met with a severe accident while returning home from this place last Saturday. His team ran away, throwing him from the grade injuring him severely. He is now at the hospital at Camp Baker, and when last heard from was in critical condition.'*
>
> *'Mr. Charles Mayn, the polite and popular grocer, of the firm of Mayne {sic} and Heitman, passed through town yesterday on his way to Baker, to see his brother.'*

I had hit pay dirt, and, for the next two years, I continued to read the *Husbandman* through the 1904 edition, mining it for all it was worth. Even though White Sulpher Springs is a small town, I was constantly amazed that these nonprominent families (Mayn and Kirchman) were mentioned so frequently and in such detail in the personal columns of the paper. The serendipitous explanation for this happy circumstance was discovered later. The *Rocky Mountain Husbandman*, which I had discovered quite by accident, has provided me an incredible forty-year history of the Kirchman and Mayn families.

### SERENDIPITY #2 - THE LETTER THAT PASSED FROM HAND TO HAND:

Just prior to discovering the article about the *Husbandman* in 1979, I had written to the Clerk of the Meagher County Court in Montana for information on the Kirchman and Mayn families. He wrote back saying he was unable to help me, but that he had passed my letter on to one of the local historians who might be able to help. The local historian wrote that she was elderly and vaguely remembered Mary Kirchman. But, since she couldn't give me any information, she had passed my letter on to one of the Mayns who still lived in White Sulpher Springs. She did, however, tell me about a pictorial history of the town. I ordered it immediately and found fifteen pictures and references to Kirchmans and Mayns.

Deryl Mayn, the third and final recipient of my letter, still lived on the original Mayn family ranch. She wrote to me shortly thereafter with information about the Mayns in particular, and we struck up a regular correspondence. I arranged to visit Deryl and White Sulpher Springs in 1980.

SERENDIPITY #3 - THE CHEST IN THE MILK BARN:

By the time I went to White Sulpher Springs in 1980, I had traced the Kirchman and Mayn families from Mecklenberg, Prussia to Washington, Missouri and then to White Sulpher Springs, Montana. However, there were gaps in the Kirchman chronology, several lost years in the late 1860's with no geographical location or other information on the family. While visiting White Sulpher Springs, I searched courthouse records, obtained oral histories from Mayn family members, located Mary Kirchman's house, and photographed everything that wasn't nailed down - cemeteries, ranch houses, and people!

During a farewell party, one of the Mayn cousins asked about the other name I was researching - 'Was it Kirchman?' she inquired. She added, 'You know, I think I have seen that name somewhere, on something. Oh yes, I believe the name Kirchman is on that old milk chest in the cow barn. I'll check it out when I get home (she lived forty miles away) and let you know.' A few weeks later after returning home, I received a photograph of a battered, beaten, broken-down, dirty yellow, three-drawer chest. Painted on the back of the chest in big, black letters was the following:

> John Kirchman
> Paola, Ks.

I couldn't believe it! Not only had I located the only Kirchman family artifact in existence, I now knew where the Kirchmans had been during the lost years in the 1860's. The very same week, I received the next two reels of the *Husbandman* and found the following in the personal column of the 28 April 1881 issue:

> 'Fred Mayn {another Mayn brother} started last week for Dillon with a four horse team. He goes to meet his brother-in-law John Kirchman and family, formerly of Washington, Mo., but late of Peola {sic}, Kansas.'

SERENDIPITY #4 - THE HOUSEKEEPER AND THE PUBLISHER:

By the early 1980's, I was using census records properly and discovered the reason why the Mayn and Kirchman families were frequently mentioned in the *Rocky Mountain Husbandman*. Louise Mayn was the widow of Henry Mayn (Mary Mayn Kirchman's brother). Henry Mayn was the brother who was thrown from his wagon and eventually died at Camp Baker. In order to provide for herself and her two children, Louise became the housekeeper for the Sutherland brothers - the publishers and editors of the *Rocky Mountain Husbandman*. Had that fortuitous event not occurred, the Kirchman and Mayn family histories would be slim indeed.

## SERENDIPITY #5 - THE RESURRECTION OF JOHN KIRCHMAN:

The personal column in the 25 August 1881 issue of the *Husbandman* revealed that:

*'John Kirchman was a passenger on Monday's coach for Helena, where he will engage in tailoring. It is his intention to set up a merchant tailoring establishment at White Sulpher Springs next season.'*

The Kirchman family never heard from John again. He had deserted Mary and their six children. Following the family story of his return to St. Louis, I began researching there for John Kirchman and his new family. This search was to continue through 1987 with absolutely no positive results. Research trips to Washington, Missouri and Washington, D.C. had provided information on John's civil war activity in the Missouri home guard, but no pension or other relevant information was available in Missouri or the National Archives.

During the Spring of 1988, I attended a conference in St. Louis and took some additional time to make another unsuccessful attempt to find my John Kirchman. After returning home, I decided just to give up on John - he was lost forever! The very next evening the telephone rang. When I answered, the voice on the other end said, 'This is Eileen St. Louis in Burlingame, Kansas. Does the name John Kirchman mean anything to you?' My heart skipped a beat - did the name John Kirchman mean anything to me? Did it ever! Fortune had smiled on me again!

## SERENDIPITY #6 - AN ARCHAIC FILING SYSTEM:

How did Eileen St. Louis find me, and what did she know about John Kirchman? After retirement, Charles and Eileen St. Louis began compiling a family history. They knew that his grandfather J. F. St. Louis had served in the civil war, so Eileen wrote to the National Archives for the civil war record of J. F. St. Louis. Within a few weeks, she received a reply from the Archives which included, among other information, the 1896 civil war pension application of Carolyn St. Louis, the widow of J. F. St.

Louis.

The pension application listed J. F. St. Louis with an *alias* - 'John Kirchman!' Included with the application was a 1905 letter from Mary Mayn Kirchman of White Sulpher Springs, Montana also asking for a pension as the widow of John Kirchman. The letter from Mary was filed with the St. Louis papers, not the Kirchman papers. And the Archives obviously didn't cross-list from Kirchman to St. Louis or vice versa. So when I searched the archives, all I found was John Kirchman's Missouri home guard record. It never occurred to me to search under the surname of St. Louis.

SERENDIPITY #7 - IT COMES FULL CIRCLE:

Eileen St. Louis wrote to the Clerk of the Court at White Sulpher Springs asking for information about Mary Kirchman. And who was the newly elected Clerk of the Court of Meagher County, Montana? Deryl Mayn, the third-hand, letter recipient, who was by now a close friend and correspondent. Deryl immediately called Eileen and told her to call me in Tuscaloosa - and then, finally, I HAD THE REST OF THE STORY!

John Kirchman didn't move back to St. Louis - HE CHANGED HIS LAST NAME TO ST. LOUIS and took the initials 'J.' for 'Johann' and 'F' for 'Frederick' as his first name. He married Caroline Bastian in Lawrence, Kansas on 27 December 1883 and had five more children, two of whom had the same name as children in his first family (there is always a bit of truth in those old family stories). He prospered as a respected, local merchant and died in 1895 of stomach trouble. He is buried in the Burlingame Cemetery in Burlingame, Kansas. His true life story was never completely revealed to either his first or second families.

To this day, John Kirchman remains partially explained and enigmatic - a handsome, charming man who was sometimes an actor, an athlete, a peddler, a tailor, and finally a successful merchant. A man who concealed his true age, the correct date of his immigration, who improved upon his war record, and was a bigamist - marrying two women with whom he had a total of twelve children. What an interesting and colorful character! Perhaps one day I will know even more about my great grandfather, John Kirchman, nee Johann Frederick Kirchmann, alias J. F. St. Louis."

# 12
## I'VE GOT A HUNCH

Besides inviting my genealogical compatriots to share their synchronistic and serendipitous experiences, I also was eager to hear their views on whether intuition had influenced their successful searches. Colonel Charles M. Hansen of Sausalito, California, sent on his thoughts:

"Intuition has not played a part in my research. As I carry a large number of problems in my head, I will occasionally while working on one of them come upon something useful in solving another problem, but I would classify this more as serendipity rather than intuition. On the other hand, I have a number of problems that I have worked on for years, lacking only a fact or two for conclusive proof. Despite all my efforts, research, analysis, conjecture, and conscious (or unconscious) thought, I have not been able to find the information needed.

A few others also acknowledged the validity of the serendipitous event, but not the intuitive nudge. But most of my colleagues did reenforce what I had found: that successful results in genealogical searches often indeed can be the product of following one's hunches as well as one's intellect. According to their letters, these instinctive nudges sometimes appear to be so subtle that they are easy to miss, but many fellow genealogists attest to their validity and even power. Brian G.C. Brooks of Hove, East Sussex, one of Britain's foremost family historians, writes,

"You mention serendipity and intuition in genealogical research. Intuitive, I suppose, I must be, because I enjoy genealogical work which uses those qualities."

Friedrich R. Wollmershäuser of Oberdischingen, Germany, has some very strong opinions:

"Intuition is a gift. And the more your mind is open and free from stress, the better it works."

Others agreed. William W. Berkman of Colorado Springs, Colorado, had spent years looking for more on his great-great grandfather Christian Bergman of Butler County, Ohio. The Federal Census records showed his place of birth as Maryland and his children's birthplaces as Maryland, Virginia, Pennsylvania, and Ohio, so many locales needed to be examined. Bill Berkman had written to the Maryland Archives for data on the family surname, but they responded months later that they had nothing. Then one night while watching the excellent PBS-TV presentation on the Civil War produced and directed by Ken Burns, a small lightbulb seemed to go off in Bill's head:

"They showed a picture of a German Reformed Church in western Maryland. I had a funny feeling about seeing that church, so for some reason I wrote to Maryland Archives again. I asked them to search records for the Bergmans in the Frederick County area, the region where the church was located. Just before Christmas, I received their response listing the family of Christoph Bergman from the registers of the German Reformed Church of Frederick, Maryland - the same church that I saw on t.v. The fifth child of Christoph found in the churchbook, with the same birthdate given that was passed down in my own family records, was Christian Bergman, my great-great grandfather!"

Joy Wade Moulton of Columbus, Ohio, sometimes has used her intuition along with good, old-fashioned logic to sort out names in her investigations:

"When I see given names, so different they stand out on an ancestral chart, I have the sense that there must be someone in an earlier generation with the same name. Such names can be key in connecting one generation to another and identifying other kin.

Barnabas is one of those names. When I saw that John

Arthur of Virginia had given this name to his second son, I was elated. Thomas and John, the names of his other sons, were so common. If I could find a Barnabas Arthur in an earlier generation, possibly I could find evidence of a relationship with John Arthur.

Two additional men surnamed Arthur were found in the same area as John between 1730-1750, Thomas and William. With further research, three generations of descendants were identified for all three men. A pedigree chart of given names only was then made to determine the number of times the name Barnabas had been used. William's first son was named Barnabas, while Thomas had no one with that name. Several of William's descendants also had this name. My chances seemed fairly good of finding an earlier Barnabas Arthur.

And so I did. Two years before John Arthur was married, a Barnabas Arthur paid a debt as part of an inventory. There seemed to be little doubt that this man was an adult, when the sons of John and William had not yet been born. My hunch was correct!"

Harry Hollingsworth of Inglewood, California, is a strong advocate of pursuing a hunch to see where it leads. He was working on his father's ancestor James Peterson (1746 - 1837), but had been somewhat stymied in his searches by what he calls "family feelings." Something had happened in the past that caused some of his relatives to try and hide unwanted facts from being discovered. However like every good genealogist worth his salt, Harry had no use for this kind of family pride and insisted on the entire truth being told:

"All I could discover about James Peterson was that his family had been divided in sympathy during the revolutionary war, some members choosing the British side, and James Peterson himself choosing the American or rebel cause. I found this story was known among descendants of several of his many children who had apparently not communicated with each other, indicating that it had been handed down for nearly two centuries. Each tradition differed from the other, yet, always, James was painted as the hero. An unchanged tradition in each family insisted that James Peterson was born a 'Sutton,' and the war problems caused his name-change to 'Peterson.' After fighting with this problem for several years, my intuition told me that something was very wrong here! And suddenly an idea hit me: *James Peterson* was the Tory on the British side! But how was I to prove it?

I was led by this strong hunch to reconsider all the documentation I had gathered during my previous years of research. I also realized that my genealogical myopia had caused me to ignore all the documents which might prove my hunch was right - the Loyalist (Tory) records. Happily, studying all these old records did indeed break the case wide open. After many years, it seemed as if a blindfold was pulled away from my eyes and brain. It turned out that Thomas Coats Sutton of Pittsgrove, Salem County, West (now New) Jersey was a British sympathizer during the revolution, serving time in jail for his views. Nearly his whole family sided with King George, including his son James Sutton and James's wife's family, the Abbotts. New Jersey sources showed that the Suttons were hailed before the Court, in absentia, and charged with high treason. But for some reason which I have never discovered, James Sutton and his brothers deserted the British cause in 1778 and escaped to safety. It was in this period of time that he changed his name from Sutton to Peterson, probably due in part to the fact that his brother-in-law Abbott was sentenced to be hanged for his deeds. James Sutton/Peterson eventually found his way to Crawford County, Pennsylvania were he raised a large family and died.

The convolutions of this true plot of history could have gone forever undiscovered but for my sudden bright light of intuition. I can't explain it, it just happened. But, to be honest, I have always had a streak of pure cynicism in me. Family feelings and patriotic preferences down through the years had almost totally clouded the true facts of the case. If I hadn't have accepted my hunch, the truth would probably have been hidden until even now. Ironically, my discovery was more of a shock than a break-through to many of my cousins. I sensed they really didn't want such a family history ever to surface. But remember, the indisputable facts were at one time fully known, even experienced, by my direct ancestor, the notable Tory-Deserter James Sutton, alias Peterson, as well as his wife

Elisabeth Abbott and their children. Was my intuition really deep in my genes waiting for a key to unlock it?

Could facts known by one's ancestor be 'stored' in his descendants to be awakened later? I have pondered this question for some time."

George F. Capes of Rochester, New York, also hit paydirt when he followed his genealogical instincts. He knew relatively little of his ancestry when he began his hobby. One of the few relics he possessed was an old portrait which he eventually determined was of his Grandfather's uncle, George C. Capes of Vernon, New York. In 1976, Mr. Capes journeyed to Vernon and found out the location of George C.'s old family home where the family had lived generations before. There was not much hope that anything could have survived in the house after all those years since many other families had resided there also. But, as Mr. Capes says, "On impulse, I just walked up on the porch and rang the doorbell."

That impulse was to open doors that would lead to the unraveling of the mystery behind the Capes family history. The lady who now lived there, after some coaxing and time, brought forth several large portrait-style photographs mounted in multi-layered frames of wood, velvet, and rococo plaster with gold-leaf paint. One of the pictures was of a young man whom Mr. Capes instantly recognized as his younger brother Edward, while another portrait appeared to be his cousin Larry Capes. Only they now had handlebar mustaches and high, starched collars and were wearing fancy velvet coats! It was a jarring experience to realize that these pictures were not of his brother and cousin at all, but of the house's owner George C. Capes and of Mr. Capes's great-grandfather Francis W. Capes. Francis had died in 1884 as a young man, only three weeks after his son (Mr. Cape's grandfather) was born. The similarities in appearance were amazing, proving that indeed family facial characteristics do reoccur over the succeeding generations.

Other family treasures were soon forthcoming, such as an old family Bible and an ancient safe belonging to Seth Capes, the immigrant ancestor. Mr. Capes adds,

"Something made me go up and ring that lady's doorbell. I had never before asked anyone about family memorabilia and have never since received anything of value other than genealogical information. I'm darned glad I did it, because I have a rewarding story to tell anyone patient enough to listen to it all. I received one major earthquake and some helpful aftershocks, thanks to following my instincts!"

Now to be sure, as experience and plain old common sense show, following one's hunches does not *always* lead to success. The prolific genealogical author Douglas Richardson of Mesa, Arizona, comments,

"I have always tried to mingle logic and intuition in genealogical research. Today I seldom notice where logic stops and intuition begins. I suppose this is what makes a good researcher. But, I don't try to analyze it. For every one of my 'hunches' which has proven correct, I've had a 'hunch' which was dead wrong. But, I try, try, try, and eventually one of my hunches pays off."

Another correspondent urged caution:

"Unfortunately, I can't provide any examples from my personal experience where I can credit a hunch with a positive result any more times than the hunch led me to a no-go. Indeed, I'm afraid that I remember several spectacular examples where my hunch was very far afield.

One concern that should be addressed seems to be how is one to deal with the researcher who says (as a friend did to me after viewing the PBS series on the Civil War), 'I know that (Captain so-and-so, seen in an episode of the series) is my great grandfather; my father looks just like him.' This is the kind of thinking ('?hunch') that has been the bane of genealogy in the past, has given it such a bad reputation in academic circles, and which the founders of the American Society of Genealogists made such efforts to replace with documentation. Who decides what makes a good hunch and what makes a bad hunch, and what do you offer the person whose hunch is 'bad' in evidence or justification for that opinion.? 'Eek!' I think, is my response to this as a potential bag of worms."

I was most eager to hear from Dr. Neil D. Thompson of Salt Lake City, Utah, editor of *The Genealogist* - the excellent journal of the Association for the Promotion of Scholarship in Genealogy, Ltd. Neil replied,

"I suspect that intuition, if not revelation, plays a greater part in all our work than we would care to acknowledge. But I am afraid that in my personal work such part as it plays is so habituated or routinized that I do not even notice it, so that, if I make an unexpected 'find', it is nothing out of the ordinary."

My own view is that my intuition can provide me with an additional source of information that I then can verify objectively. I echo newsman Dan Rather's opinion on the subject, as cited in *Sixth Sense*, a fascinating study by Laurie Nadel, Ph.D.: "I believe in hunches, gut feelings, and intuition," says Rather. "I also say to myself, 'A good reporter follows his hunches but doesn't report them.'" In other words, according to Dr. Nadel, a good reporter checks out his hunches to find out if the *facts* back them up!

As it is with reporters, so should it be with genealogists. Dale J. J. Leppard had a recurrent, gnawing idea that just wouldn't go away:

"Perhaps the greatest surprise that I have received in the course of my research came from my investigations of my maternal family tree which stems from the isolated mountain village of Montemurro in southern Italy. I think most people (myself included) tend to stereotype Italians as devout Roman Catholics which, for the most part, they are. However, this region was also populated at an early date by Greeks as well as refugees from the Byzantine provinces of Palestine and Egypt and even Moslem invaders.

I had discovered that my 5th great-grandparents were Domenico Zaccaria and his wife Caterina di Mose, both born in 1731. The latter surname 'di Mose' in Italian means 'of Moses.' As soon as I saw it, I felt there must be a Judaic origin behind the name, but quickly dismissed that idea since, after all, this was a Catholic family living in Italy! Somehow, I just couldn't forget about it, so I finally went to a local college library where a study of the naming patterns of the area led me to the logical assumption that this Moses was a Jew. But what would a Judaic family be doing in a remote mountain village in southern Italy?

I sent a battery of inquiries to Christian and Judaic researchers, archivists, and historians all over the world to try and find the answer. As their replies came in, a pattern clearly developed: everyone seemed to agree that the surname 'di Mose' had or probably had a Judaic origin, but my correspondents also all expressed reservations about the presence of a Judaic family in the region! Finally, a Professor in northern Italy, the leading authority on Italian Judaic history, answered. He located an old record concerning gold collected from southern Italian Jews for the coronations of the Spanish Kings Alfonso I and Fernando I in 1459; among the Judaic communities listed as having contributed was none other than the little village of Montemurro! Another letter from another expert told me that Montemurro was actually founded by the Moslem Saracens over a thousand years ago, who in turn gave Jews more rights and privileges there than did the Christians. The Jewish community was still flourishing in the village in 1459, but was forcibly converted to Christianity in 1540.

My hunches as to a Judaic origin for my ancestress then were correct. But I cannot explain what drove me to pursue such an admittedly bizarre possibility, nor can I explain why I was driven so hard that I sent inquiry after inquiry to three continents to find an answer. Why didn't I just give up when all the initial replies questioned the presence of Jews in a rural Italian mountain village? I don't know, but I couldn't rest until I had received the information about the Judaic community in Montemurro. Only then did I feel I had completed my quest and, in this instance at least, my perseverance was definitely rewarded. And maybe, if you believe in such things, this finally explains why I have always had a curiosity about Judaic culture? Sometimes I just 'know' something is right, or where to look, even though it may seem quite fantastic or improbable. I think the 'di Mose' story illustrates that quite well!"

Instinctive hunches often can permeate one's entire attitude towards research. With Judge Eunice Ross of

Pittsburgh, Pennsylvania, they take the form of a general skepticism toward glib pronouncements of some German and American writers as to how exactly the American branches of her Latshaw/Lotscher family descend from the Swiss family. Some older publications stated that her forefather Johannes Franz Latschar was descended from one Hans Heinrich Latschar, a Mennonite of Kuhborncheshof near Kaiserslautern in the Palatinate. After immersing herself in original sources here and abroad, Judge Ross has been able to disprove much of what earlier genealogists erroneously affirmed. The serendipitous findings of an old newspaper clipping and then a 1713 German lease confirmed what her instincts were telling her all along about her family. It turned out that Johannes Franz was too old to be son of the Kuhborncheshof man, but instead escaped persecution in Wittgenstein by fleeing the country in the 1720s. When she leaves the bench, Judge Ross plans to pursue her hunches further and try to unravel even more of the complex Latshaw/Lotscher riddle. She comments:

"Perhaps your successful searches have been the result of your extraordinary sensitivity to your own collective unconscious. I do not believe everyone has it, and some have it more than others. But I do believe that most successful genealogists have, on occasion, that flash of knowing plus the serendipity of finding things that unlock hidden mysteries."

Maurice R. Hitt, Jr. of Binghamton, New York, spent years looking for the origins of his immigrant ancestor Henry Hitt, who first shows up in Stratford, Connecticut marrying Sarah Bassett in 1673. After years of searching earlier records for Henry, nothing still could be found previous to his marriage. It seemed to be an impenetrable obstacle. Exhausting most of the primary records without success, one day he happened on an obscure book *A History of the Town of Greenwich, Connecticut,* by Daniel M. Mead in which an account of a Reverend Jeremiah Peck was noted. It said that Peck was a proprietor of Elizabethtown, New Jersey, and moved to Connecticut because of the violence due to the quit-rents. As Mr. Hitt recalls,

"It was no more than two lines in the book, and I didn't think much of it at the time. But as the day went on, that little nugget of information kept nagging at me, seemingly telling me to look in the New Jersey records. Finally giving in to it, I started browsing through *The Colonial Records of New Jersey*. There for the love of God was my Henry Hitt, listed as a servant for the first governor of New Jersey. That opened up a whole, new world, and I have since discovered data on the family back to 1398 in Devonshire, England!"

Rabbi Malcolm H. Stern of New York, New York, recalls an intuitive thought that propelled him towards the successful resolution of an old problem:

"I remember an incident from my years in Norfolk, Virginia. In a history of the Jews of Richmond, I found a reference to a circumcision of 'Moses, son of Uri Feis' in Norfolk in 1795. For years it stayed as just a miscellaneous note in a notebook, until I came across another Uri Fice who anglicized his name to Philip. The bulb went on! Moses, son of Philip, whose father could have been Moses might be an allusion to a well-known Revolutionary soldier, Philip Moses Russell, who had been a surgeon's mate at Valley Forge for the 2nd Virginia Regiment. My intuition became fact when I was subsequently shown a family Bible in which Philip Moses Russell's son was recorded as being born in Norfolk in 1795!"

Sometimes a hunch can be the gentlest and simplest of nudges to look in a particular place or do something a certain way. To Douglas L. Haverly of Loudonville, New York, it was just a gnawing feeling that the old family tradition that his ancestor Henrich Hager had come to America with four brothers and their uncle Pastor Johann Friederich Hager was erroneous; Doug's detailed research over the years finally proved the old tale was indeed wrong.

In 1989, Mary A. Pitts of Sacramento, California, was looking through scattered issues of *North Irish Roots*, a publication of the North of Ireland Family History Society. Knowing that she had Irish forefathers in her Potter and

Stewart lines, she looked for an index to the magazines, but there was none. She relates:

"As a normal rule, I don't peruse periodicals if they don't have an index, but, in this one instance, I did. One article I looked at contained the report of a talk on the Stewarts of Ballymoran by a Mr. Jim Stewart. My own research had indicated that possibly my family could have originated there. I was able to get hold of Mr. Stewart by letter, and eventually he sent on much material on both my Potter and Stewart families, who were indeed from that village, as well as the surprise via documentation that we were even related to each other. This exchange opened up even more leads, which, in turn, led to finding other relatives and more ancestors here and abroad.

I can't say why I carefully checked those few issues that we received in our library page-by-page. It was just one of those hunches you get. It still is hard to believe that, out of those few periodicals, they would contain just the clue I needed to help me find my Potters and Stewarts in Ireland!"

Ervin F. Bickley, Jr. of New Canaan, Connecticut, feels a combination of intuition and subjective deduction certainly played a part in finding his ancestors.

"I first became interested in genealogy about 1950 through a cousin who searched the Bickley line for some time past. She had proved our line for four generations but had been unsuccessful in connecting it to a Bickley family of English origin which had been in Philadelphia since colonial times. Since I got my start from her, I, naturally, focused on the English connection and spent untold hours in this effort also without success.

After some years of failure, there arose to the surface the recollection and thought that since childhood I had heard a lady who lived in our area and who attended our church called 'Cousin Lydie.' She was then in her 80's, but I went to see her and asked her how we might be related. Without hesitation, she told me that her grandmother and my great-great-grandfather were half brother and sister.

With that clue, I was able to locate the true connection

which was not English at all. My family came to Philadelphia in 1732 from Schwaigern, Germany, having gone there from Töss, Switzerland about 1660. I have since traced the family name 'Baggli' in Töss to the 13th century. All from an idea, or stroke of intuition and the recollection of an old cousin."

I have come to believe we all have this "sixth sense," and that our intuition can be nurtured and developed. Interestingly enough, a high IQ seems not to be a requisite for being a sensitive (although, of course, many very bright people have achieved successful results when they tap into their intuitive nature). Researchers Robert and Henie Brier tested several samples of individuals who belonged to the Mensa Society (sole qualification for membership being an IQ within the top 2% of the population) and published their results in "ESP Experiments with High IQ Subjects." In all the tests of ESP by Mensa members, their average score was significantly *less* than expected by chance.

Sometimes the "gift" of psychic powers almost seems to pour out of the sensitive person. Helen Harriss of Pittsburgh, Pennsylvania, probably has contributed more stories to this book than anyone else, and there may be a reason for this. She writes:

"When I was a student at Ohio State University, one of my professors in a psych course asked if he might be allowed to test us for ESP. I think it was in connection with the research being done at Duke University. It did turn out that my senses were quite acute, and he asked me to continue with a series of experiments - the usual things like recognizing cards which were face down, etc. He did tell me that I tested high on the scale of their research. I never thought much of it or really used it very much. But I have enjoyed it when it occurs in my research. Anything that helps is fine with me!"

Carol Willsey Bell can certainly attest to Helen's gift. Carol remembers:

"Back in 1976, I was involved with the BiCentennial Conference on American Genealogy held in Cleveland. I agreed to lead a post-conference bus tour to Columbus to the Ohio Historical Society, and to lecture on the bus while we were enroute. One of the passengers was a French Canadian who stopped me before we went into the library. He said he was trying to find a recent book written by a lady named Turk (I think her name was Margaret) about some French Canadian families. He knew that she was a resident of the Cleveland area in the suburb of Parma, and had hoped that the Ohio Historical Society might have a copy of the book. We checked the card file, but, alas, no copy was there. I promised that I would try to help him when we got back to Cleveland.

I was rooming with my good friend Helen Harriss of Pittsburgh. I told her the story of this man's quest, and grabbed the Cleveland phone book in the hotel room. Turning to the name Turk, I was dismayed to discover one entire column of that name, and certainly no one named Margaret! Deciding that I needed to know which prefixes covered Parma, I checked the front. Nearly every listing for Turk was in Parma! Now what to do? I handed the phone book to Helen, and watched her run her finger down the list. She stopped at one name, and said, 'Call this one.' I did, and a lady answered. I asked her if by any chance she was the author of the book on French Canadians, and she said, 'Why, yes I am!' Once again, we hit the jackpot!"

Helen Harriss herself expands on this story:

"What is inexplainable to me is that I do have a 'Tingle' - for want of a word, which I often feel when going down a list of names, running my finger over the list. Suddenly, I do feel this weird sensation - and almost always, it is the name I need. In Carol Bell's case, I swear that I had never even met the woman - I knew nothing of that surname - but when I ran my finger down the listings, there was a definite feeling on one entry. Carol was daring or desperate and decided to try it out. It *is* hard to believe, but it was the woman's number. Carol looked as if she were seeing a ghost when the woman answered and identified herself as the author of the book. This trait has been a big help for me in researching, as you can guess. It doesn't always happen, but the odds are pretty good that it will!"

Many people find it hard to acknowledge and accept gifts

such as Helen possesses. The old values die very hard. So many of us still cling to the tenets of the Newtonian revolution, which enthroned causality as absolute ruler of matter and mind. Everything *had* to have a logical cause and effect, and, if it didn't and couldn't be explained, its worth was negated. As Dr. Laurie Nadel reflects in her book *Sixth Sense*,

"Most of us are conditioned not to make full use of our intuitive abilities. In fact, many of us are conditioned not to rely on them at all. From earliest childhood, we are praised and rewarded for performing mental feats involving logic, memory, and other measurable cognitive skills. The entire foundation of our traditional education system is predicated on the belief that these skills are superior to other mental abilities such as imagination and intuition, which can be experienced qualitatively but which do not lend themselves to the same kind of quantitative measuring as do memory and logic. In other words, intuition cannot be tested and measured in the same way as arithmetic can be tested. Thus you learn early on in life to program your mind to use only a limited part of its ability in performing all its tasks. It's as though you were taught how to drive with the advisory to use only your frontal vision and to exclude your peripheral vision.

It's so sad. Many of us were brought up to believe that nonrational means irrational. Irrational, in turn, implies emotional, out of control, and possibly even crazy!"

But finally, we are awakening. The times - they are a changin'! The validity of the unconscious and its impact upon our lives has been established by psychiatry. And other branches of science have followed suit in opening up new avenues of exploration. As Arthur Koestler so eloquently states:

"The odor of the alchemist's kitchen has been replaced by the smell of quark in the laboratory. The rapprochement between the conceptual world of parapsychology and that of modern physics is an important step towards the demolition of the greatest superstition of our age - the materialistic clockwork universe of early-19th century physics."

Apropos of this as we look at intuition, it is helpful to remember that what was yesterday's folly is today's fact! Until the thirteenth century, man did not realize that he was surrounded by magnetic forces; they've been proved to exist, but we still have no direct sensory awareness of them. And until the mid-19th century, hypnosis was treated as an occult fancy by Western science; today it has become so respectable and commonplace that we are apt to forget that we have no explanation for it.

The whole nature of the process of discovery is an intriguing area for thought and reflection. Jane Fletcher Fiske reflects:

"Certainly as genealogists we should apply every scientific standard we can to our research and our work. In our efforts to be scientific, however, we should not lose sight of the fact that many of the greatest discoveries in science have been first conceived through the vision of minds open to intuition. I'm not advocating ouija-board genealogy, but I am not arrogant enough to believe that I can understand all there is to know, even about my own field, and I don't really want to. Life is an ongoing mystery with volumes yet to be written, and if I thought I could achieve total rational control of even my corner of it, the world would cease at that moment to be interesting."

Jane echoes the views of the great Albert Einstein, who placed a high value on his intuition when he wrote:

"The intellect has little to do on the road to discovery. There comes a leap of consciousness, call it intuition or what you will, and the solution comes to you, and you don't know how or why."

Former NASA astronaut Edgar Mitchell, who conducted in-flight experiments in ESP with professional psychics back on earth with a success rate far greater than predicted by chance, founded the Institute of Noetic Sciences upon his return to study this phenomena. Mitchell has stated his belief that "the psychic component of the intuitive function, that is, the ability to perceive information in ways unexplainable, is a natural part of the universe. It is available to everyone."

Dr. Jonas Salk, inventor of the first polio vaccine, in his book *Anatomy of Reality: Merging of Intuition and Reason*, gives a good deal of credit to intuitive thinking for his successes in scientific research. In order to obtain good results, Dr. Salk sometimes would visualize himself as a particular virus and then intuitively sense how that virus would behave. He observes:

"I feel as if this is all occurring at a level of my mind that I sense to be beneath consciousness and that seems to want to merge with my conscious mind. At the moment when the two converge, when they commune, I feel a rush of ecstasy, a sense of release, of satisfaction, of fulfillment."

I certainly can identify with Dr. Salk's feeling of elation! As I mentioned earlier, I made a conscious decision to trust my *un*conscious and follow my hunches in my Palatine searches. And the more all these 18th-century families became "family" to me, the higher the success rate I attained in documenting their ancestral homes overseas. By immersing myself in the lives and times of the Palatines, in a sense I became one with them - just as Dr. Salk did with his viruses.

Many of my associates endorse this approach, and state this experience is absolutely essential in order to make genealogy really "work." Brenda Dougall Merriman comments:

"When I lecture, teach, or advise clients, one of my biggest goals is to *put the descendant in the ancestor's shoes*: his location, his surroundings, his family, his social context, etc."

Dr. Duncan B. Gardiner of Lakewood, Ohio, feels the same way:

"If I have a genealogical project which allows extensive and intensive research, then I try to learn *everything* about the circumstances of the people involved, trying at each step to visualize how they lived, and especially how they emigrated: Geography, economics, social structure, routes, destinations. At a certain point, one accumulates enough data to see patterns connecting a population in Europe with a population in North America.

There is not always enough data to see the patterns clearly, but the accumulation of knowledge gives one a 'feel' for the situation, an intuitive grasp of the families involved. Moreover, the intensive sifting of information and records over the span of a number of months undoubtedly is worked over by an investigator's unconscious calculator, and this process could eventually surface to the conscious mind as intuitive insights. Intuition is given to us after accumulating adequate data and having the knowledge allowing us to accurately picture our ancestors' lives at each important point in time."

C. Frederick Kaufholz of Lakeville, Connecticut, has spent most of his genealogical career tracing generations of families in the German town of Duderstadt. He knows them all! Fred remarks,

"You are quite right, that intuition plays an important part in genealogy. It goes without saying that after what I call the educated guess, there comes the proving of it. After 65 years in genealogy, I have become fairly good at the educated guess. It was not until 1964/65 when I made an intensive study of the archive of Duderstadt that I began to appreciate how much I had learned without knowing it!"

Kenneth Frederick of Lake Forest, Illinois, writes,

"The goal of my about-to-be-completed 15 year effort has been to identify all descendants to the eighth generation of all the German families who came to Guilderland, Albany County, New York ca. 1738. I immersed myself in Albany County records as well as materials from Schoharie and adjoining counties. In retrospect, I see that intuition did play a role in how I progressed, step by step, but all unconsciously."

Peter Stebbins Craig of Washington, D.C., adds his comments:

"I have had remarkable success in following hunches in my own work - hunches that are rooted in having first wallowed among a particular ethnic group of immigrants. In my case, I have been concentrating on the 'Antient Sweeds' of the Delaware (as William Penn once described them) - those settlers who peopled the colony of 'New Sweden' on the Delaware 1638-1655, with a couple of shiploads more arriving 1656-1664 under Dutch rule. Having discovered or verified my own New Sweden roots (as set forth in my article "The Yocums of Aronameck in Philadelphia, 1648-1702" in the *National Genealogical Society Quarterly*, Vol. 71) I became curious about the entire group. But I met a stone wall when I compared names on the New Sweden rolls of 1638-1655 with the names that appeared after the English became established on the Delaware. Where did these 'new' Swedes come from; what happened to the 'old' ones?

The first step, of course, was to recognize that the Swedes came to this country steeped in the tradition of using patronymics, not surnames. This helped in tracing Jonas Nilsson's sons to the Jonasons, later Jones; or Constantinius Grönberg to his son Conrad Constantine. But others defied analysis. Where did some come from, and to where did others disappear? Patronymics was only part of the answer. I needed to immerse myself into that society, know all of its families, and how they thought. First names became more important than last names. I had to trust my hunches, recognizing that in the society I was looking at, only first names stayed constant."

Mr. Craig then goes on to give marvelous examples of how studying all the families in New Sweden and trusting his own intuitive knowledge of the group unravelled many problems that had puzzled genealogists for years.

Marsha Hoffman Rising of Springfield, Missouri, ponders the complexities of this whole intuitive/serendipitous area:

"I can certainly relate to the 'passion' and all-consuming nature of one of these community ancestral projects. I become so absorbed in trying to find my 1000 Springfield Land purchasers that I actually resent *anything* that intrudes - such as eating, sleeping, and people I live with. Hunches and instincts do become important, but do we experience them because of accumulating knowledge and 'living within the community and among the people'? Is it because of the amount and breadth of the research that we create 'this pool of knowledge' for ourselves? Or do we 'inherit' it?

Usually when I find someone in a place I didn't expect, it feels like serendipity rather than intuition. I am actually <u>looking</u> for someone else. But because so many of these people have entered my consciousness, I recognize the name and the associations. So, rather than intuition, it often appears to me it is the breadth of study. But I am not sure.

Therefore, I have challenged three of the most difficult people in my Springfield study. I have said to Joseph Weaver, C.D. Terrill, and Littleberry Hendricks ...'If you want to be in Hank's book, I am waiting for a Twilight Zone experience that will lead me to your origins.' If any of my three lost sheep take up my offer, I will send it along to you!"

COME ON, YOU THREE SPRINGFIELD SETTLERS ... I'M *WAITING!*

## 13
## PRAYERS & DREAMS

As I've mentioned, the diversity of opinion as to the "whys" of serendipitous and synchronistic events is as fascinating as the occurrences themselves. Some colleagues approach this whole area from a purely scientific frame of reference and dissect each experience as if it were a laboratory experiment. Other family historians, no matter what their religious affliliation or orientation, firmly and simply attribute their successes in making genealogical discoveries to a spiritual source.     For example, June B. Barekman of Illinois, one of the driving forces behind the Chicago Genealogical Society and one of the most beloved members of the genealogical community, had an astounding experience while searching for her ancestor:

"Thinking back in time, what I experienced was not a hunch or "Twilight Zone" event either; it was my answer to a problem put there by a power greater than me. My 3rd-great grandparents were (Georg) Peter and Anna Ursula Bergmann/Bargmann/Barrickman, who married in the Palatinate in Germany in 1746. They arrived in America in 1749 with two children and settled in Frederick County, Maryland. When Anna Ursula died, Peter married a second time in Maryland to an Elizabeth and moved with his new family to the area near Vincennes, Knox County, Indiana by 1783/84.

One of my major goals was to find the will of Peter Barrickman in Indiana. Box "A" of the Knox County Court Records noted that his will was made in January of 1791 and probated in September of that year. However, that file box didn't contain his actual will. I thought that perhaps it had been sent to Indianapolis for microfilming, but a check of those records revealed that it wasn't there either. I then offered a $200.00 reward for the first person to find that old will, but there were no takers. Over a period of six or more years I kept returning to Vincennes and eventually searched every file and box in the recorder's room in the basement but with no luck.

After all those years of fruitless searching, I was very discouraged. On my last visit there I sat with my head in my hands, feeling hopeless. Where was that will? I decided it was time to go back to Chicago and forget about the will of Peter Barrickman. I stood up and walked aimlessly around the room. I wandered over to a far side of the room and idly pulled open a drawer that had no bearing at all on my needs. And there was the will of Peter Barrickman!!! It had been removed, put into a new file envelope, and placed in the back of this drawer, why I will never know. It was over two hundred years old when I finally found it. I held it to my cheek, tears running down, and thanked Providence for giving it to me. It now resides in Vincennes on display for all to view. Since finding that will, I have completed full genealogies - some short, some long - on the seven children of Peter and Anna Ursula, and five fair-sized studies on the children of Peter and his second wife Elizabeth Barrickman."

Mary Smith Fay of Houston, Texas, has a prayer group that meets every Friday. They discuss a chapter in a book they have all read for about thirty minutes and then spend the next half-hour making lists of special prayers needed for situations in the world, for friends in need, and for themselves. Mary remarks:

"This is the highlight of my whole week. Sometimes the prayers are for the short term also. As a genealogist, I was appointed by the Harris County probate court to determine all the members of a family who were in line to inherit. Sometimes this is called 'searching for missing heirs' or 'forensic genealogy.' A young Houstonian had married a girl from Galveston; but, when he died about six months later of influenza during the 1918 epidemic, the obituary mentioned no wife but 'two little daughters,' not named. Because I could find nothing about the two daughters in Harris County, I went to Galveston to search. Before I left, I asked the Prayer Group to pray not only for a safe journey but for a 'mini-miracle.'

My first stop was at the Galveston County Courthouse, but there was nothing in the probate records mentioning the last name of the family. Very disappointed, I said to the clerk helping me, 'Let's look under the mother's maiden name.' Sure enough, there was her last name, followed by the word 'minors.' As the clerk got down the heavy volume referred to in the index, I told her I had asked my Prayer Group to pray for a mini-miracle. When she placed the book on the table, she didn't even have to turn a page! The book opened to the desired page; facing me was the entry about the 'two little daughters.' An uncle of theirs had died, and they were named in the estate settlement because their mother was not living. Our next stop was upstairs to look at the loose papers in bundles which are accumulated when an estate is settled. This case wasn't settled until the 'little daughters' were grown and married. I came away with not only their first names, but also with their married names.

God had indeed wrought a miracle!"

Kathleen T. Rasmussen of Mountain View, Wyoming, was on a trip to Germany, looking for her ancestress, Elisabetha Wohlgemuth, in the village of Oberlaudenbach where she was "supposed" to be born. But by the time she arrived in the region, she had just one day left of her European trip to do her searching. As she remembers,

"I told my Heavenly Father that I desperately needed his help. I just didn't want to go home empty handed. After 3 hours of trying to find the village, we stopped at a gas station to ask directions. But we spoke no German, and it seemed a hopeless task. However, another customer who did speak English was there, filling up his tank. He was expert in lay of the land, and gave us excellent information on how to get to Oberlaudenbach. Why did he just "happen" to be there at that gas station on that particular day?

On his advice, we stopped at the Catholic churches at Oberlaudenbach and Laudenbach. But both were shut up tight. You can imagine how hurt I felt. However, just across the street from us was seated the second answer to my prayer. He was man with a broken leg who spoke no English, so he had his wife call a young high school girl to translate for us. As it happened, this man's best friend was a local historian, who knew the secretary of the Catholic Church at Heppenheim - where the records were kept. Of course, our interpreter had nothing to do that day and was willing to tag along with us, as the historian spoke only German.

We consulted lots of records, including school files looking for an Elisabetha Wohlgemuth born 7 October 1857. Unfortunately, she was not there. But all of a sudden, our interpreter started jumping up and down. She had found an Elisabetha Lulay with the same birthdate. Further investigations proved that she was indeed my Elisabetha Wohlgemuth, born as an illegitimate child to Elisabetha Lulay. I received full data on her family, visited her ancestral home, and eventually was able to know her entire story. That particular day, I must have had my prayer answered at least five times, as doors opened enabling me to find my great grandmother and her family.

And it hasn't stopped! I've continued to have many wonderful experiences where I've come up against a blank wall, but then miraculously found my way through it!"

Morris A. Shirts of Cedar City, Utah, had a family tradition that portrayed his ancestor, Peter Shirts, as a faithful member of the L.D.S. Church. In discussing his forefather with a local expert on the Cedar City area, his friend recalled that he had read something somewhere about Peter Shirts's "disfellowshipment" from the church. but didn't remember exactly where he had read it. In the interest of accuracy in chronicling his family history, Mr. Shirts made the finding of such an entry an important agenda item for his next research trip to Salt Lake City. He writes:

"When I arrived there, I went directly to the L.D.S. Archives Library and began working on all the microfilms that might hold the information page by page, flicker by flicker. At the end of the first day without success, I told my wife, 'It's not productive. I'm tired and don't feel like spending more time at this.' But the next morning, I had a feeling that I should try again, so we postponed our return home. I returned to the Archives and checked out more journals and reports. But by noon, I had 'had it,' turned in the materials, and headed for the restroom (I was suffering one of the effects or symptoms of diabetes - the urgent need to visit the men's room all too frequently).

After relieving myself, and while washing my hands, I felt a strong impression to pray. Realizing what a consternation it would cause if someone came into the men's room and saw me on my knees, I decided to face a corner, standing up, leaning on both walls, in prayer. While thus engaged, goose pimples erupted on my forearms, tears came to my eyes, and I had a strong sensation in my chest. At first, I thought I was having a heart attack; but instead, I made a fast and excited walk down the hall to the research area and asked if the material had been returned. The receptionist said 'yes, but not all of it has been refiled yet.' She retrieved these for me. There were five or six journal-type books. I picked up the one on the top of the stack and began to pass the pages through my thumb and forefinger. I saw the words 'Proposed that Peter Shirts ...' I was so excited that I could hardly turn the pages looking for that statement, and at last I came to it! In the minutes of the St. George L.D.S. Stake dated 9 November 1873 was indeed a notation that we 'cut off Peter Shirts of Pinto Ward ...'

Our family files were corrected to show he was cut off, but eventually he was reinstated on the official records of the church ... Was this an accidental thing that I stumbled onto in the hundreds of pages I scanned? No, I don't think it was. I attribute it to Divine guidance and an answer to prayer rather than to intuition."

If indeed divine guidance is a factor in this great mystery, then it appears one avenue of helping us is through our dreams. Dreams can be the windows to our soul ... just ask thousands of psychologists ... and me! The more I began chasing my beloved Palatines the more I began to dream about them. Sometimes an 18th-century emigrant would appear in my dreams and yell at me, "You're looking for me in the wrong place ... look for me over here (in this other region) instead!"

At first, I ignored these bedtime intrusions, writing them off as undigested remnants of too many pepperoni pizzas. But they appeared so often during my sleep that I eventually began to pay closer attention to the content of their messages. I felt compelled to stop making searches in certain areas, change course, and seek the emigrants elsewhere. And lo and behold, many times my researcher Carla did hit genealogical paydirt in the very villages where the dreams suggested we look!

Barbara Baxter of Southern Pines, North Carolina, remembers:

"I decided to take on the project of tracing my family history because I was an only child, my mother had been an only child, and no one else would do it. My mother died about twenty years ago, and, when I cleaned out her things, I uncovered a box of various materials. Some of the papers my grandfather and grandmother Button had collected, including some old letters from relatives. I knew that none of my children would even recognize most of the names and was lamenting the fact that I had never questioned my forebears about specific family matters. It made me sad that my great-grandmother, whom I knew well, had been born about the time of the civil war, yet I had never really learned anything from her about the family history.

Shortly after that time, my mother came to me in a dream. After talking with her about the mundane things like 'I miss you,' she responded that it was nice where she was and she would very much like to come back, but that they wouldn't let her. I thought to mention some of the family names that I had heard discussed as a child and asked who they were. She explained how all these people were related, and then the dream was over! Whether I had these facts in my unconscious from childhood, or whether she actually did communicate them to me I have no idea. However, this 'conversation' did help me in some of the research that I would undertake fifteen years later when I semi-retired."

Ejvor Merkley of Mesa, Arizona, relates:

"I remember a dream I had while in Pennsylvania. During this dream, I walked into a small country church, and, as I stood there looking towards the pulpit, a door opened in the back. A short gentleman walked down the aisle and asked me what I wanted. I told him that I was looking for records on a certain family that belonged on the Stapley family line. Then I realized that in my arms I was holding their large family history book. The man looked at it, and then said that the material they had in the book was wrong! That was the end of the dream.

I had no intention of working on this particular line because it had been researched by many people, and I felt it had been done correctly. Still, for some reason, the next morning I told my children that we were going to Allentown. Searching courthouses and cemeteries was not their idea of a fun vacation, but, with the right kind of prompting or bribery, they agreed to help. I went to the courthouse in Allentown because I felt it would be a simple matter to find the crucial Stapley ancestor's will. In the will, he would list his children with their married names, and that would be proof that this woman in our line did indeed marry the man we had her married to. After an hour of searching, my son Richard said, 'Mom, this looks like the right will. The man's name, death year, and the names of his children all match the list you gave us, but this daughter Catherine isn't married to the right man.' After checking it very carefully and finding that it was the right family, I decided Catherine must have had two husbands. It didn't take long to find Catherine's husband's will (the husband mentioned in her father's will), and, lo and behold, he was living during the time she was supposed to be married to the person on the pedigree chart I had.

To get more information, I asked directions to the church where I knew the town cemetery was located. I told my kids that we'd just check a few gravestones. It was way out in the country, and, by the time we arrived, a light rain was falling. I decided to go see if I could find someone inside the church to tell us where we could find the graveyard records. I'm sure you can guess what happened next. I started walking down the aisle trying to get someone's attention, when I noticed the door of the chapel open and out stepped a short man. He walked down the aisle towards me, and I stopped and just stood there. He told me his name and asked what I wanted. I said that I was tracing this particular family and had the records in my car. He told me that I was at the wrong church and that the family I wanted actually was buried at a church several miles away. He said it happened to be the very family *h e* was descended from also, that the information the Stapley family had on their charts was wrong, and that he had the correct information at his home. He then drove to his home and returned with the charts and documented materials I needed.

I have my own feelings about this experience, as it's very special to me. It happened for a definite purpose and made a real impact on my life. It helped me realize the importance of finding the truth about family relationships."

Ken D. Johnson of Grand Island, Nebraska, had a fascinating experience relating to a genealogical dream:

"I have for sometime believed that there is some guiding force behind our genealogical finds. I personally saw very little use in doing genealogy until my grandmother told me that my grandfather, who had been in a coma for just over three days, awoke about an hour prior to his death and asked for her to 'tell Kenny to keep my family together.' These were Pa's last words. My grandfather (Pa) and I had been on the outs with one another for about sixteen months over my becoming a Mormon, he being a staunch Baptist.

Approximately two months after his death, he came to me one night in a dream. In the dream, we spoke no words to one another. He just extended his hand to me, and I felt his strong grip and warmth. He then showed me in the Bible where what I had chosen to believe was correct and true. It was shortly after this visitation that I embarked on my career as an amateur genealogist. I know it sounds crazy, but my grandfather was there, and we met in the flesh. The man who I admired more than any other person I've ever known told me and asked me to do what I am now doing. I know this is hard to believe, but I know it to be true."

Paul I. Edic of Akron, Ohio, has a story to tell:

"I had a dream one night that I thought was very

fanciful. I dreamt that I had opened a book, and there, plainly in black and white, was printed precise information about my immigrant Ittig ancestors and their exact place of origins in Europe! I woke up thinking, 'what a nice dream, but it was only a dream.' Less than ten years later, you came out with your work *The Palatine Families of New York - 1710* followed by *The Palatine Edicks & Related Families of New York,* by Philpot and Conrad, just a few years later. My dream had come true!"

Of course, some dreams can be a bit diabolical. Gordon L. Remington of Salt Lake City, was working for a client on the man's civil war era ancestor in the Stoneman family. It had been a largely fruitless and frustrating search. After this negative investigation had gone on for some time, Gordon had a dream in which his client's elusive ancestor kept hiding from him, then poked his head out to reveal himself, only to hide again. The man even teased Gordon by saying, "Ha - Ha! You're never going to find me!"

That did it. When he awakened, Gordon was very angry and all the more determined to find additional information on this person. Within a few weeks, his tenacity paid off, and Gordon discovered a wealth of data on the man.

There's a moral to this:

NEVER TAUNT A DETERMINED GENEALOGIST - *EVEN IN A DREAM!*

# 14
# *HOME AGAIN*

My colleagues report that returning to the geographic locale where an ancestor once resided often can produce strange experiences. Professor Mark L. Wahlqvist feels a deep affinity with his ancestral Swedish locale whenever he visits the region:

"My relatives still live in the highly traditional, even mystical part of Sweden between the 1,000 year old North-South Road and by beautiful Lake Salen, with two 'meeting circles' of stones 2,000 years old and burial mounds from the late Viking period about 1,000 A.D. Our ancestors almost certainly used these stones and are buried in these mounds as the number of families who live in the area are still few. Tradition is still strongly maintained by our relatives there. The sense of connection that I personally have with the place is profound and restorative, making it one of my most sought-after destinations. It is, one might argue, a kind of spiritual connection and the basis of good intuition."

I know what he means. One of the great thrills of my own life was finally visiting the lovely regions back east where the Palatines had settled. A life-long California resident, my first trips to the Hudson, Mohawk, and Schoharie Valleys in upstate New York fulfilled a longing deep inside that is hard to describe. It was almost as if I was "home." But the wild thing about my first visit to "Palatine Country" was the intense feeling of a geographic *déjà vu* which I experienced as I traveled through the beautiful countryside. Several times, I literally knew what was around the next bend of the road as we drove along - even though I had never been there before! Some of this could be attributed to my intensive reading about the locale, but it wasn't an intellectual process I was going through. I would see mental pictures of what lay ahead which would then be proven true as I turned the corner of the highway.

Ms. Marty Hiatt of Lovettsville, Virginia, remembers a talk given by Tucker Withers to members of a Loudoun County historical society recently that reenforces just how strongly a locale can "call out" to a descendant. Mr. Withers had decided to move from Bethesda, Maryland to Middleburg, Virginia (a distance of no more than 40-50 miles). After much looking, he found some property there that was ideal for his proposed antique shop. The real estate agent told him that he had to come back to his office in the nearby small community of Aldie, five miles from Middleburg, to sign the final contract.

Upon his arrival in Aldie, Mr. Withers struck up a conversation with Mr. Cockerill, an older resident of Aldie. The elderly man blurted out, "I know you ... you're Cleve Wither's boy!" Mr. Withers was astounded. His parents had divorced when he was three years old, and he had lost all contact with his paternal relatives. As it turned out, his father and grandparents prior to their deaths had been long-time residents of Aldie. Through simple chance, Withers had chosen as his new hometown his father's old hometown! Marty Hiatt says, "I think Tucker Withers was led home by his ancestry. He knew at once that Aldie was the place for him!"

Dr. George Moore of White Stone, Virginia, has had several rather jarring events occur while searching for his Mor/Mohr forefathers in Austria and Germany. He was following up clues that suggested that Andreas Mohr of the area near Nassau, Germany originally might have been a refugee from the vicinity of Innsbruck, Austria. He had traced several prominent lines there back to one Heinrich der Möre who had come from Zernez in the Engadin Valley to Innsbruck in 1331. On his first trip to Austria, Dr. Moore decided to center his investigations then in the area of the South Tyrol near Zernez. He and his wife thought it would be nice to find a castle hotel in the middle of the region to use as his base of operations during his searches. They found a book on castle hotels and found three in the South Tyrol to choose from.

Then, as he says:

"A miraculous event took place. For some unexplained reason, we picked the Schloss Labers Hotel just north of Meran in the area. We arrived at the hotel quite tired from our largely unproductive digging. It had been cold and rainy in Zernez, and that day we had traveled over high mountain passes by bus and train before we finally reached our destination. The castle hotel seemed warm and cozy as it welcomed us at dusk, and we sought the comfort of our reserved room in the castle tower after we registered.

As we climbed the red-carpeted wide staircase under crystal chandeliers, we came to the first landing where the stairs made an abrupt turn and paused to catch our breath. On the high walls of the landing, there were various medieval weapons and armor displayed along with banners and tapestries. My wife suddenly pointed to a massive wall hanging and said, 'George! Look! There is a painted family tree of the Mor family.' I was somewhat skeptical that a Mor wall hanging would be located in this castle, but I examined the tapestry and found the name of Thomas Mor of Zernez upon it!

Needless to say, we were both excited. The next day, I asked the hotel owner if I might examine the tapestry carefully and perhaps even photograph it. He was most kind and had his staff place a twenty foot ladder on the landing so that I could examine it closely. The wall hanging was about five feet wide and about twelve feet high and offered a complete line of the Mor family descendants from Heinrich in Zernez. I was able to copy a continuous line of ancestors back in time to the 1300's and even document that the name Mauer was indeed a variant spelling of Mor as I had thought. It also provided the evidence I needed to link the Austrian and German families together. We were absolutely elated at our chance find! When I had finished, I returned the ladder to the hotel owner who had been quite amused by my antics in full public view. I asked him where he had obtained the tapestry. His reply was that he had been at an auction at a castle in Schluderns looking for items to decorate his hotel and simply bought it as a decorative piece! Could the ghost of the Mor who painted the tapestry some two hundred years ago have guided our 'chance discovery' or was it pure chance?"

Dr. Moore experienced another curious event which unnerved him on a subsequent trip to Austria. He was visiting the old manor house of Hieronymus Mor at Dietenheim near Bruneck. The house was called "Sonnegg" and was built about 1550. As Dr. Moore recalled:

"The owners of the house were most generous and made us feel at ease when we asked if we could explore the manor. Entering that cold, gray building gave me an excitement that I had rarely experienced before. Somehow, I felt as if I had been there at some previous time. Every room seemed vaguely familiar. When I looked at the walls and ceiling, I saw frescoes painted as if they had been done yesterday. There were religious paintings from the Bible and depictions from Greek mythology. Most interesting were the coats-of-arms painted across the higher walls of the large dining hall. Hieronymus had painted the Mor family crest each time that one of his seven children was married along with the family crest of the new family, if the son or daughter-in-law had one. The owners finally persuaded us to sit at a huge wood table and partake of some wine.

As I sat there, I just could not get over the impression that this entire experience was one that had happened before. Even my poor German seemed to become more fluent. And I remember that thoughts of my father and grandfather kept entering my mind. Although both were dead, my impression was that they were also in the room. I shall never forget that experience and have often wondered if the owners of Sonnegg would allow us to spend a week there by ourselves."

Evelyn S. Wache of Palenville, New York, can understand Dr. Moore's feelings:

"One thing I've noticed is that places I've been drawn to locally often turned out to be those connected to my 'roots.' I've always loved the Embought area along the Hudson in Greene County as did my father. He never realized what I have come to know, that those lands were settled by his ancestors. I also was always drawn to the little old Palenville cemetery, which in my early years was sadly neglected and overgrown. As far as I knew, none of my forebears were buried there. Then I got hooked on genealogy, went back to that restored cemetery, and found a gravestone honoring my own great-great grandparents there. Further exploration turned up yet another marker of my great-great-great grandfather in the same cemetery!"

Helen L. Harriss remembers a fellow-member of the Western Pennsylvania Genealogical Society who had gone with her husband on a trip to Germany. They fulfilled a life-long dream by visiting the town from which his family had emigrated many years before. Upon their arrival, they stopped a passerby on the street to ask directions to the local church. A conversation ensued, and the stranger asked the couple their names. Unbelievably, it was also *his* name, and he turned out to be a distant cousin also vitally interested in family history. After personally showing them the church, the man took them to meet relatives still living there. It was a wonderful reunion which would not have happened if they had asked just any other stranger!

Similar events happened to Edward Reimer Brandt of Minneapolis, Minnesota. He writes,

"Talk of serendipity! On two occasions, the very first person I talked to in a European village (once on the street, once in the cemetery) turned out to bear one of the names I was researching. In one case, it was a flight attendant who just 'happened' to be at home momentarily; in the other case, it was the wife and mother of the only three men in a sizeable village who still bore what was once a common surname there."

Maralyn A. Wellauer of Milwaukee, Wisconsin, remembers:

"When I peel back the layers of my genealogical experiences looking for those most inexplicable, I find it difficult to sort out which of the many occurrences to discuss. Countless times I have read almost illegible handwriting to decipher the name of an ancestor; turned to pages without mindful purpose to find a tidbit of information; chose the correct name from the many until real proof was available; or pulled a book randomly from the shelf to find some unexpected treasured bit of information. Some ancestors have seemed to leap off the pages, while others have assumed a 'personality' before me as I copied their vital statistics. I have grown very fond of many individuals on my family tree this way. I am grateful to all these peculiar experiences in my twenty-five years of genealogy and consider them some of the perks of the profession.

But perhaps one of the most moving experiences in my life happened in Switzerland several years ago. On a visit to Stein am Rhein, the town where my great-grandparents lived before they emigrated to the U.S., I reserved a room at a small hotel - mostly because it was the closest to the railway station and my baggage was too heavy to carry any further, and partially because it was a short distance down the road from the town archive, my planned stop to do family research.

The hotel was moderate in size, comfortable, and reasonably priced. It was very quaint in appearance, being an old half-timbered building with a slanted roof, and had many rooms. On what was to be our last full day in town, my parents, my aunt, and I walked out of the door together. On previous occasions, we were all on different schedules and so left at different times. My mother, the first one out the door, gazed upward and was surveying the building when she said, 'What was the name of the family you are going to look for? Isn't it Buel?' I replied that it was. She said, 'Well, that name is etched into one of the stones of our hotel, above the door to the left.'

Sure enough, a memorial plaque, set when the house was renovated, proclaimed this as the birthplace of Johannes Buel, the brother of my 4th great-grandfather, who was a native-born diplomat who had gained quite a reputation in local history. Of course, I copied down every word and then proceeded to the archive to finish my work. Shortly after I got settled, I came across a biography of Johannes Buel which was shelved without reference in the card catalog. I paged through the book and found pictures of my 5th great-grandparents and a sketch of their home, which also served as an outlet for the family bakery business. It *looked* like our Hotel Rheinblick, and *it was!*

I then proceeded to find out all the information I could about the building, and eventually was able to reconstruct a complete house history. I found it was home to my 5th great-grandfather - a baker, councilman, and hospital director - his second wife, and their 27 children (who fortunately were never all domiciled at the same time). I also learned many family stories about my ancestors who had lived there. For example, how my Johannes was born in so weakened a condition there that the housemaid suggested throwing him into the Rhine River as one would dispose of a young cat; and then how he was saved due to his strong facial resemblance to his father. Many of the details of life in that old house were moving to read and a challenge to 'experience.'

When I returned to the Hotel late that afternoon, I roamed from room to room to get a feeling for what had happened there so many years ago. The owner even opened up unoccupied sections, storage areas, and crawl spaces for me to view. I mentally noted every nook and cranny in the living space, and tried to imagine how it was back centuries ago. I felt so fortunate to find out that this had been my ancestral home and felt blessed to be able to sleep there.

Thank goodness I made that trip when I did! For when I returned to Stein am Rhein the next year, I was dismayed to find that a major renovation had taken place. The Hotel was now a drinking establishment called the 'Sherlock Holmes Pub."

In 1987, Nancy Vannoller talked her husband into taking their vacation in Marietta, Ohio, where her father's Alcock family had settled in 1797. She had discovered through correspondence that there was an Alcock family cemetery there and wanted to investigate it. Upon arriving, she recalls:

"We visited the local library where we found a map in their genealogical section showing various cemeteries in the area, including the Alcock cemetery. Piece of cake, right? WRONG!

We drove for miles, up and down the road, trying to find the place. We even went back to the library to see if we had misread the map. Back on the road again, we found lots of cemeteries and lots of Alcock graves, but not the one we were looking for. Nor could any of the caretakers we talked to help us.

Finally, I told my husband I was just going to stop at a house in the area to see if anyone had ever heard of this Alcock family cemetery. Needless-to-say, he thought I was nuts. But we stopped at a big old farmhouse I liked the looks of, and I asked the young lady in the front yard if she had ever heard of this cemetery.

Not only had she heard of it, her house was the Alcock homestead, and her Dad's mother had been an Alcock! She called her Dad, who lived next door, and we spent the afternoon talking and looking at old pictures. There was even one of the original house built by our mutual grandmother Sarah and her four sons in 1798. Along with those marvelous pictures, he had the lock and key from the original house which was torn down and replaced about one hundred years ago.

Oh yes, the Alcock cemetery where Sarah was buried that we tried so hard to find: someone had bought the land in the 30's or 40's and plowed it under. We never would have found it."

Dorothy Craig of Rancho Murieta, California, wanted to someday see the ancestral land where her 9th great-grandfather Richard Parrott/Perrott Sr. settled in Middlesex County, Virginia in the 17th century. On an excursion in 1989 with her Society, she went to the area in that old county where a 1669 map showed a small creek called "Perrot's Creek" flowing into the Rappahannock River. Like any good genealogist, she was hoping that this geographic landmark might be an indication as to her forefather's residence.

Mrs. Craig went to the local post office at Jamaica, Virginia and asked the lady working there if she had ever heard of a Parrott's Creek or knew of anyone of that name who lived nearby. The woman did not, but suggested that Mrs. Craig should not waste her trip and still should see the beautiful countryside and the Rappahannock anyway. The lady gave complex directions about where to turn and just which fork in the road to take to reach the river.

After Mrs. Craig had traveled several miles in the back country, she came to an unexpected fork in the road and had absolutely no idea where to go. There was a two-story white house directly in front of her, so she went in search of someone who might be able to give her directions to get to the river. As no one answered the front door, she went around the back of the house and found the most beautiful rolling green lawn and pastureland which ran down to a boat dock along the Rappahannock River. A person who was at the far end of the pasture saw her, and they started walking towards each other. When they met, Mrs. Craig explained that she had come from California all the way to Virginia looking for a creek named Parrott's Creek. The lady seemed very surprised and said, "Parrott's Creek runs a short distance south of here, on the other side of the old family cemetery. But, madam, you have come to the very house which Richard Parrott built in 1649!"

Mrs. Craig was, as she says, "speechless!" The lady then gave her the "Grand Tour," showing her family treasures, old pottery and Indian arrowheads from the vicinity, and even ancient throw rugs with bloodstains on them from the time of the revolutionary war when the house had been used as a hospital. It was a dream come true.

Donna J. Porter of Denver, Colorado, had a memorable experience in 1966 while she and her husband were searching in Clarington, Monroe County, for her great-grandfather.

"We had been to the cemetery there, and I was disappointed at not finding his grave. It was about dusk and, as we drove back through the residential area of town, no lights were on in the homes along the street except for one, single house. We could see an elderly lady sitting in the window reading.

On a total whim, my husband suggested that I go knock on the door and inquire if she might know of my great grandfather. After thinking it over, we both decided to go, as one person alone might frighten her. We knocked on the door, and, when she opened it, I told the lady that I was looking for someone who used to live in the town named 'Bishop' (my maiden name). She smiled and invited us in immediately saying, 'Come right in, this is the old Bishop house!' We spent a delightful evening with her, enjoying her stories of the town and of the Bishop family who once lived in her home."

Dr. Bernd Gölzer of Stiring-Wendel, France, shows this phenomenon can even happen to professionals working on a client's line:

"Last year I was very deeply involved in searching a certain family of foresters in Kindsbach, five miles west of Kaiserslautern, Germany. My client was an American descendant of the family who especially wanted to find his ancestral home. I drove through Kindsbach and, as is my practice, took lots of snapshots of houses and streets in the town.

One house I liked especially well, and I thought to myself that this would certainly have been a nice place for the emigrant to live in. It was half a year later that I found a document made by a notary public which dealt with the emigrant's property sales prior to his leaving Germany. The old record showed that the American's ancestor had lived in exactly that same house that I had fancied!

Strangely enough, this story repeated itself yet again on another occasion. I was searching another German line for this same American client, and the same thing happened in a village in Upper Alsace where I also had never been before!"

Anna Harvey had a Bible record giving the names of her grandmother's brothers and sisters. Fortunately, she knew the area of Canada where the family lived, just over the border from Swanton, Vermont. So she took this sheet of paper with her on her first visit to Stanbridge East, Canada, home of the grandmother's family. Not knowing where else to go for information, she went to the local historical society there. The president of the group took one look at the paper and excitedly told her, "My grandmother's sister married your grandmother's brother. We're relatives!" Through the kindness of this lady, Mrs. Harvey extended her Palatine line far back in time, became acquainted with other relations, and even was able to see the old gravestones of her grandmother's family.

Dr. Duncan B. Gardiner of Lakewood, Ohio, was once investigating materials in the Kosice archive in Eastern Slovakia. As he tells it,

"While there, I met a Doctor researching his genealogy. We chatted and exchanged ancestral names. 'Krupitzer?' he said, 'I know a Dr. Krupitzer living in Poprad.' I replied, 'Oh, all my family left for America, they must be one of the other families by that name from the town.'

A year later I followed up on the contact, meeting the doctor and his parents. They turned out to be my third cousins. I spent a weekend with them, and they told me the story, still vividly remembered, of how my great-grandfather Albert had sent a steamship ticket to his great-grandfather, a cousin. The family story was that Albert was a very powerful, strong blacksmith.

This was a chance occurrence, but it depended on following a clue which at first seemed unlikely to produce interesting results - which is another lesson experience teaches genealogists!"

Dr. David Faux of Hagersville, Ontario, has long had an interest in the military side of both history and genealogy. Besides tracing the "paper trail" which documented his ancestors genealogically, he also tried to flesh them out and discover all he could about their uniforms, the weapons they used, and what accouterments they might have carried into battle. As he was interested in archaeology also and had published articles in the field, one of his dreams was to locate the original house site of his revolutionary ancestor, John Young, and assess what physical traces still remained. His project soon met with success, thanks to surviving maps and surveyor's notes which led him to the precise location. David recalls:

"I can remember thinking to myself before arriving at the site, 'wouldn't it be marvelous if I found items that were actually used by Lt. John Young, and wouldn't it be awesome if I could find a military artifact that he actually

Military artifacts found at the site of John Young's home.

carried with him during his long service?' The realist in me said that the chances were infinitesimal since, even accepting that his son or grandson might have tossed something like that out on the trash heap, my chances of ever finding it were almost non-existent. The probability was so low since I would only be doing a surface collection, and any real 'goodies' would in all likelihood be buried six feet down in the bottom of the old cellar.

Well, and again this defies my rational explanation, among the items churned up by the plow which I picked up on the surface of the field were two seemingly non-descript things that, however, looked familiar to me. After studying my books at home, I realized that I had uncovered a sword pommel (the ball-shaped, butt-end of a sword) and a wrist escutcheon from a Brown Bess musket that predated 1790 (matching its counterpart in a reproduction of this weapon that I had hanging on my mantle).

To think that I held in my hand two items that were likely carried by an ancestor into battle over 200 years ago is quite enthralling. Again, considering my intense interest in the possibility of finding some military trappings owned by an ancestor at the time of the revolution, and realizing that scouring the antique shops would be futile since the items seldom if ever have a documented history included, and knowing that no one in the family is known to have inherited such items, what were my chances of holding something in my hand that John Young had carried with him into battle?

They have to be as close to absolute zero as one can get. And yet, I was drawn toward that field with an eager anticipation that it was at least possible that I would find some small artifact that could be attributed to the man. What force allowed me to overcome reason, logic, and awareness of the odds and, in a determined way, forge ahead and locate a tangible link connecting me to an an ancestor who was born 200 years before my birth? It's kind of spooky, and I really don't know what to make of it."

Sometimes an ancestral locale can turn out to have an unexpected bond between modern-day descendants. Wallace and Sylvia Van Houten of Middleburg, New York, met as young students at Michigan State University. They were married in

Michigan, lived there for a few years, and then finally settled in lovely Schoharie County, New York, when Wally was offered a good teaching job there. Like most young couples, genealogy and family history was not of much interest. But after twenty-five years of marriage, the genealogy bug bit hard and, wonder of wonders, they learned that many of Sylvia's ancestors as well as Wally's had lived in Schoharie County right where they now resided. Documentary evidence also indicated that many of their mutual forefathers, such as Wally's Nehrs and Sylvia's Dygerts, knew each other back in the early 1700's from the date of their arrival in the colonies with the great Palatine immigration. By 1723, their families all dispersed to other locales, such as the Mohawk Valley of New York and Tulpehocken, Pennsylvania. But, as Wally believes, in a sense they all met again in 1952 in Michigan and, in 1958, came home again to their Schoharie County origins!

# 15
# GHOSTS, PIXIES, &
# THINGS THAT GO BUMP IN THE NIGHT

But sometimes the stories shared by my colleagues almost seem to find their roots in another dimension. Herlinda Taylor Carney of the Ventura County Genealogical Society in California had one of the most remarkable experiences I've ever heard of in genealogy! Her story has been well known on the west coast for the past decade, but, as is so often the case - like in the kid's game of "telephone," has been modified and changed in the telling as it was passed along from genealogist to genealogist. After searching long and hard to find her, I finally tracked Mrs. Carney down and was able to obtain the correct story as it occurred. As she tells her tale:

"This happened to me when I was still a novice in genealogy, having done about three or four years of research. One morning, I was at home cleaning the tile in my shower stall. I was almost finished and was working hard, doing the floor. All of a sudden I looked up and saw a piece of plaid cloth, which I would estimate was about eight inches by fourteen inches, pass above me. I was absolutely stunned, but I did manage to note the colors of the material.

I forgot all about the incident until months later when I was home preparing my research notes for a trip to the Los Angeles Public Library. All of a sudden I noticed a cloud of cigarette smoke right next to me. This was extremely strange, as I have never smoked in my life nor did anyone else living in my house at that time. This phenomenon reoccurred several times thereafter.

When my lady-friends picked me up the next day to go to the library, I laughingly mentioned that perhaps they wouldn't want me along on the trip. I then told them of the experiences I had had the previous few months. My friend Darlene asked me to describe the plaid, which I did to the smallest line and detail I could remember. When we arrived at the library, Darlene didn't say a thing, but snuck away from the group. She went to a corner of the reading room and had a book pulled on the Scottish Plaids and Tartans. When we examined the volume, we found that I had precisely described the Bruce Tartan.

I was in shock because my great grandmother was named Catherine Bruce! I knew very little about her as she had died when my paternal grandmother was ten years old. All we really knew about her was that she had been a schoolteacher. I knew that Bruce was a Scottish name, but I was a novice then and just had not thought to look up a Tartan. This strange incident was the motivating force in getting me to start my search for Catherine's ancestry.

But I am a great believer that there is a certain time, the "right" moment, to find these ancestors. For Catherine remained an enigma for twenty years until 1990 when a lady I had done some research for finally found my great grandparents' marriage record in Meigs County, Ohio. A few months later, I casually mentioned to an acquaintance that I had met six years earlier that I was going to look for my Catherine Bruce in earnest now that I knew about her Meigs County origins. Fortunately, the lady knew the family well, as her great-great grandmother was sister to my elusive Catherine Bruce. Finally, after all my years of looking since the plaid first 'appeared,' I was able, with the lady's help, to document my Bruce family back to Virginia and then Scotland.

When I called an aunt of mine and told her about the plaid story, she said to quit doing all that research. I responded that I wasn't afraid of the dead, only the living!"

La Fay Eastman Gowan of Hoover, Alabama, related a wonderful story to me in a recent letter:
"In 1980, my son, daughter-in-law and I planned a trip to England. My family reluctantly agreed to grant me a few days to take a trip to Redruth in County Cornwall to do research on my Eastman family and see just where they

came from. Before leaving, my husband Jack purchased a watch for me and made me promise to wear it. I never wore jewelry on my arms as it always bothered me. However, I promised Jack I would wear the watch, and I agreed with him that this one time it was necessary to have a time-piece with me.

The agent at the train station in London looked confused when I asked to purchase tickets to Redruth. I had to show him where the village was located on a map and that train tracks appeared to go through it. After checking further, he explained that Redruth was not a regular stop, but there would be no problem in them making a special one for us. The next day we boarded the train south, finding the journey delightful and the scenery captivating. The further south we went, the less reluctance I noticed in my companions.

Upon arriving in Redruth, the one and only taxi was awaiting us, as news of the train stopping there had preceded us. The taxi took us to the beautiful hotel, Penvention, that had been converted from a Manor House. We had found the real England, not the tourist's England. Everyone was so gracious and accommodating, really reminding us of the real Southern Hospitality. That evening, the pianist entertaining during dinner even played 'Dixie' and 'Stars Fell On Alabama' to our delight. Incidentally, we could understand the Cornish accent better than any place we had been in England; it was more similar to our Southern accent.

We visited the small library and Town Manager. Then we went to the church where my ancestors had been buried. A lovely young milk-maid (with a bucket of milk in each hand!) strolled by and chatted with us. She informed us that the older cemetery from the earlier era of my forefathers could not be maintained and was now overgrown with thorny bramble bushes. We could only take a photo of the present church, knowing our ancestors were somewhere nearby. I had found some information on my family and had made contact with a gentleman living in Redruth, Joseph Eastman, who had the same given name as my great-grandfather. However, I had not really come upon any exceptional discoveries on my kin.

The next day we boarded the train that made a special

stop for us at 10:20 A.M. and traveled back north toward London. After boarding the train, I looked at my watch, and it had stopped on 10:20 - the exact time we left Redruth. I shook it and tapped it, but it just wouldn't work. It stayed on 10:20. I put it in my purse as I was tired of wearing it anyway. During the rest of our visit to England I would check the watch regularly when I would open my purse, but the hands remained on 10:20.

In London, I made an appointment with a well-known genealogist regarding some research in Great Britain. During our conversation, I happened to tell him about my watch and how it stopped as I was leaving Redruth. He laughed at me and humored me by explaining that people from the States just could not accept the fact of 'Little People!' He explained that my watch was not broken and not to have it repaired. He said the 'Piskies' stopped it to tell me that there was more information to be found in Redruth, and that I was leaving too soon. (I put two and two together and realized that 'Piskies' was Cornish dialect for 'Pixies.')

The day arrived for us to return home. Just as we flew over Ireland and started our flight over the Atlantic, I opened my purse and, by habit, looked at my watch. And behold - it started running and then continued to run without any problem. In my first letter to the genealogist after arriving home, I told him how my watch started running again. His return letter to me explained that my watch was definitely 'enchanted.' The 'Piskies' let me go because they knew I would come back one day.

Two years later, my husband Jack and I returned to Great Britain. This time I wore my watch, just in case there was something to these 'Little People' called 'Piskies.' Why take chances!!?? Of course, Redruth was again on our agenda. We stood on the spot where my ancestors home was. We toured all of Cornwall, but really my actual research was not genuinely successful. We journeyed northward to County Devon where my ancestors were living even earlier. Still no real success, but we really enjoyed touring the county, and I met more Eastmans (although connections were probably so far back that much research will be necessary to make any firm connection).

At the train station the day we were leaving Devon, we

strolled up and stood by a quite distinguished lady. We struck up a conversation between us that was startling! She immediately asked us if I were not a genealogist. I answered 'yes.' She said she was from Australia, researching *her* family. At that point the train arrived. We three boarded it and continued our conversation. The family names she was researching meant nothing to me nor mine to her; however, I gave her a compiled pedigree chart of mine and my husband's, as I had brought several copies with me. We left the train in about an hour, saying our goodbyes and exchanging addresses with this delightful lady. We then continued onward north to Scotland, homeland of some of our other families.

A few weeks later we arrived back home to find a letter waiting for us from that nice lady from Australia. WE WERE RELATED! Our distant grandmothers were sisters! I immediately named my watch 'My Enchanted Watch' and mailed it to my newly-found cousin in Australia. I explained that one day I knew it would return to me in a very unusual way. I'm just waiting for my 'Cornish Piskies' to make their move. Maybe your letter, Mr. Jones, was instigated by them. We shall have to wait and see. (Written this third day of March in the year 1992 while five Pisky statuettes watch over me and my research)."

Jane Adams Clarke of Philadelphia, member of the Board of Directors of the Pennsylvania Genealogical Society and editor of its newsletter *Penn In Hand*, had an experience she will never forget:

"One night, about ten years ago, I woke to a whirring or whistling sound. When I opened my eyes, I saw standing by my bed a woman. She was, I would say, in her 50's or 60's. Although she was dressed in black (black bonnet, and black dress), she had a very vivid complexion. She had flaxen colored hair pulled across her forehead so that it showed under her bonnet; vivid blue eyes; and rosy cheeks. She was frowning at me. I knew immediately that she was angry, but I had no fear of her.

As far as height is concerned, she was just as tall as my bureau ... one inch short of three feet; however, I did not see her feet, as the lower portion of her body was hidden by my bed. Could be she was floating.

I immediately sat up and stared at her. I was wide awake. She did not move, nor did she say anything. My dog was at the foot of my bed. I looked at him to see why he wasn't barking, but he was asleep. When I looked back, the lady was gone!

After a bit, I went to sleep. Later in the night I heard the same sound, but did not open my eyes, as I was afraid of what might happen next. I've often been sorry that I didn't open my eyes, as I would like to know why she appeared. Although I have been told the spirits often haunt the places where they have lived, I think she was related to me, and if she was, she had not lived in this house, as I have only been here since 1970. She bore a striking resemblance to my father, his siblings and his mother. They had flaxen hair (although most had curly hair ... her hair was very straight); they had china blue eyes, and a ruddy or rosy complexion. Also, she had a squarish face, which is a family characteristic. The family is short in stature ... my grandmother was only four foot eight.

I have many family pictures, but her countenance, which I will not forget, has not been found in anything I, or relatives have. At this time period, I was most involved in my family research and had several problems in finding my people. No doubt I had gone to sleep with these problems in mind. I think she appeared as I had found something she did not want to be revealed, or perhaps I possibly had misplaced her in the family. At the time, I was having much difficulty (and still am) finding something out about my great-great-great grandmother Delilah; however, this is my mother's ancestor, and the coloring and family characteristics don't fit ... as far as I know.

I have a tin photograph of a very old woman ... born in the mid 1700's. I am having difficulty placing her as I have conflicting family stories. She was thought to be Delilah ... but I think she was Delilah's mother-in-law. Perhaps this is the problem.

Perhaps, this was my great-great-great grandmother on my father's side. She was born in Germany, and came to this country with her husband and children in 1818. This woman did have a child born before her marriage ... and perhaps this was the problem. Family members I have met

in Germany have the same coloring and facial features as
my father's family.

Whatever is bothering her, I wish I knew! Perhaps I
have resolved the problem, and that is the reason she did
not return. I do know that I saw her!"

I am very open to Jane's story, as I had my own brush with
what might be called "The Other Side" a few years ago when I
first began my explorations into the psychic arena. Never
much of a "joiner," I decided one evening not to work on my
Palatine volume, but instead to take a chance and see what a
meeting of the respected Southern California Society for
Psychical Research would hold. I had read some of their
thoughtful and insightful *Journals* and *Bulletins*, written
under the leadership of such noted scholars and investigators
as Raymond Bayless and Dr. Elizabeth McAdams. They were
famous for their efforts at debunking charlatans and
separating the flakes and phonies from the genuinely gifted
psychics via their stringent tests and experiments.

I knew no one, and no one knew me when I arrived for my
first meeting with the Society on February 5, 1979. As I
entered the room alone, several individuals were conversing
quietly in a corner. All of a sudden, one of the group, a lovely
young woman in a long, flowered-print dress, whirled
around, pointed her finger at me, and said loudly from across
the room, "You're writing a superb book! Don't let it go to
your head!"

That was my introduction to the Society and to Leslie
Newman, the psychic who was to be evaluated that particular
evening. Needless-to-say, I was astounded by her words and
eager to know what would happen next. I didn't have to wait
very long. A few moments later, during the general psychic
readings which were being monitored and tested, she startled
me by turning and asking, "Who's Raymond?" I couldn't think
of a living soul I knew of by that name, so I replied, "I have no
idea." Leslie Newman responded with, "Sure you do, it's
somebody's brother." I thought for a second and then froze in
my tracks. "My God," I realized, "*I'm* Raymond!"

One of my closest high school friends was Judy Watson,

THE DRAMA DEPARTMENT
of
San Leandro High School

C. BURRELL, Superintendent     L. CRITSER, Principal

Presents

## KISS AND TELL

COMEDY IN THREE ACTS
By. F. HUGH HERBERT

### CAST

(In order of their appearance)

| | |
|---|---|
| *Mr. Williard* .............. | Don MacDonald |
| *Louise* .................... | Maryanne Bull |
| *Corliss* ................... | Judy Watson* |
| *Raymond* ................... | Hank Jones* |
| *Mildred Pringle* ........... | Coleen Calhoun* |
| *Dexter Franklin* ........... | Wally Cole* |
| *Janet Archer* .............. | Joan Yarosz |
| *Harry Archer* .............. | Bob Conrad* |
| *Pvt. Earhart* .............. | Dick McLain* |
| *Lt. Lenny Archer* .......... | Roger Thompson |
| *Mary Franklin* ............. | Shirley Brown |
| *Bill Franklin* ............. | Larry Bern |
| *Dorothy Pringle* ........... | Mildred Jessup* |
| *Uncle George* .............. | John Ravekes |
| *Robert Pringle* ............ | Mel Hughes |

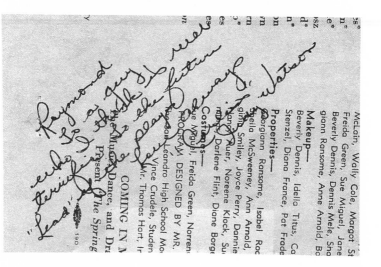

Setting the stage for a visit from the other side.

with whom I appeared in the senior play "Kiss And Tell." In that production, Judy played "Corliss Archer," and I was cast as her younger sibling. Throughout the rehearsals and performances, and then afterwards for the rest of our high school years, Judy wouldn't call me by the name of "Hank," like everyone else did. She endearingly used my character's name from the show instead. It was a private nickname, a secret, special bond between us that no one else knew. Judy always called me her "Little Brother Raymond."

To tell you the truth, I hadn't thought much about Judy for years, and she certainly wasn't on my mind prior to the reading. We had gone our separate ways after high school, and really only kept in touch with each other via Christmas cards over the holidays. But I do remember being shocked and saddened in the early '70's when her brother Tom telephoned me to relay the terrible news that she had died of a brain tumor, much too young, survived by her husband Dick and her children. She was the first of my school-days contemporaries to go, and her early death was a real tragedy that hit me quite hard. Other than some older relatives who had passed away, Judy was the only really close friend I knew who had died.

Was she trying to reach me from another dimension "beyond the veil?" I was dumbfounded and amazed, because there wasn't another soul on earth who knew that special coded name of "Little Brother Raymond" which only Judy and I shared between us!

Judge John D. Austin of Queensbury, New York, recalls:

"Marcia, my wife, and I obtained our long-time residence in a way unconnected with any family ties. I was serving as Town Supervisor in Queensbury, and we were renting an apartment, anxious to have our own place. The Town Bookkeeper and her husband were building a new home next to their present brick residence, and she told me that the old place was for sale. Marcia and I looked at it, liked the house and the neighborhood, and made the move. Next door to the brick house was a historic old stone dwelling. The Bookkeeper's mother resided there by herself. The Austin family was growing, and after we had been in the brick house a year, the Bookkeeper's mother decided she wanted a smaller place and asked us if we would trade houses. We did so, and have been here since.

Marcia's ancestry, including her maternal O'Leary line, focuses on Glens Falls, a city a few miles south of us. A brief sketch of my great-great grandfather Austin in an 1876 county history mentions work in the hotel business, which I believed must have been in Glens Falls, and I knew that his long-time farm was on the other side of Queensbury. In short, neither of us thought we had any close family ties to the neighborhood of our brick house and our stone house.

Soon, however, I became interested in the history of the old stone house and the neighboring properties. I put together the census entries, deeds, mortgages, and probate records for the locality. I discovered: (1) The long-ago owner of my stone house had foreclosed a mortgage on a tavern just down the road. (2) He sold the tavern (hotel) to my great-great grandfather Austin, who operated it for seven years. (3) During that period, the acreage between the stone house and the tavern was owned by farmer Michael Lary (O'Leary), Marcia's great-grandfather.

On March 2, 1980, a skilled psychic repaid me for the preparation of her will by doing a 'reading' in our stone house. She asked me why I was so interested in the neighborhood, and I told her about the discovery that my ancestor had operated a tavern nearby. Thereafter, she went into various trances and related a multitude of interesting and believable past visions of the house and its occupants.

Towards the end of the session, she looked at a portrait over the fireplace.

'Is that your great-grandfather?' she asked.

'Yes,' I answered.

'No,' she said, and went into a trance. '*This* man did *not* have a tavern out here. He resided and did business on Glen Street in Glens Falls. He wrote his 'f's' in the old fashioned way. He was very indulgent to one of his daughters. He loved to hunt partridge. He wanted a substantial new bridge built across the Hudson River at Glens Falls. He made small business loans to people he could trust.'

I was astonished. She was absolutely correct. The portrait was not of great-great grandfather Austin, but of another great-grandfather, a man named DeLong who had all the attributes that she specified.

Would that I might find a 'genealogical psychic' who could go into a trance and come up with some of those missing maiden names on my charts!"

One of the most amazing stories shared with me in the course of this project came from a widely-respected, very well-known genealogist with impeccable credentials. Although she allowed her name to be used in connection with several other incidents in this book, she asked that this particular experience be presented anonymously. As she says:

"It's too 'far out.' I have told it to a few people - only ones I knew would not think me crazy!"

My friend continues:

"When I was a child, my grandmother lived with us, and my bedtime stories were often of events of her childhood or stories which had been told to her by her parents, etc. They were good, well-told, and sparked my interest in doing genealogy as well as my desire to be a history teacher. Of course, I did not ask enough questions. I recalled the events, but not the name of the aunt or uncle or cousin who was involved. As I researched the family, however, the clues were valuable and led me to fill in gaps and often to locate the person who had been involved in the incident.

One of my grandmother's maternal families had come from Maryland. I had visited the place where they had lived in the 1600's and 1700's, and my name was on file there. Therefore, I was not surprised to hear from a man of that surname, asking for help in searching his family, who had moved to Missouri from their home near Chambersburg, Pennsylvania. I checked for him and found the family in the 1860 census, just a bit before they left. I sent him the information along with some other data that I found. However, I still was not sure of the relationship to my family, except from the surname, a not-too-common one.

A few weeks later, while I was in church on Sunday morning, something seemed to be coming into my mind - some unfinished business about that family. I put it in the back of my thoughts and began driving home. All of a sudden to my astonishment, there was 'my grandmother' sitting beside me in the car - as real as in life (she'd been dead for almost

30 years)! She appeared as 'solid' as I did - although I did not dare touch her. She said, 'You should have remembered what I told you about that,' and it was her voice, as clear as when she used those same words to chide me when I was a child.

Just as suddenly, she was gone. But the story she'd told and that I'd forgotten was in my mind, as clear as if she'd just told it to me. It was that just before the battle of Gettysburg, these relatives of my great-grandmother's had heard horses hooves passing their farmhouse near Chambersburg. They got up and looked from their window, seeing Confederate soldiers riding past the house. They wakened their son - then about 12 - and sent him across fields, a back way, to warn the Union soldiers of the approaching southerners. The boy did not return, the story goes, and the family was worried that he'd been captured or killed. They heard the loud cannonfire of the battle, so the men did not go to the fields to work, but instead guarded the family at home. The battle over, the son returned and told of the adventures he'd had hiding to watch the battle.

That's all to the story, but it's interesting to note that my correspondent's family did have a boy of the right age to have been that one. My husband also assured me that the cannon were of types that would have been heard where these people lived, and it's logical to think this was the family.

It was a very eerie experience. When I came home, my husband asked, 'What happened? Is the car all right?' I was still shaking. In fact, for several days, I quivered. Luckily, nothing like it has happened since!"

**Carol Boice Jones De Paul of Pittsburgh, Pennsylvania, writes:**

"I've wanted to share the following story, 'BOICES - ON AND OFF THE WALL,' with as many people who would listen. Everyone I know has heard it, and I was beginning to stop strangers on the street to tell them! Even after 18 months have passed, I find myself still shaking my head in disbelief:

It was during the fall of 1989 that I had absolutely given up hope of ever locating the parents of William Boice, my great-great-great grandfather. In fact, I had given up hope of even locating William. It seemed he had disappeared from the face of the earth ca. 1826.

What I had discovered during the previous 25 years was that he had probably been born in the 1790's, served in the War of 1812, had married Priscilla McMichael (1797-1855) in August of 1816, had six children - Nancy, Ellen, Jane, Mary, John McMichael Boice (my great-great grandfather) and Robert W. Boice - all born between 1817 and 1826. And, it was possible that he was related to an Ebenezer, a cabinetmaker and justice of the peace whose office (in 1825) was in his house, above a blacksmith shop in Burgettstown, Pennsylvania. This small country town is located about 20 miles or so from Pittsburgh. Even though my mother felt that we had no Boice relatives in the Pittsburgh area, I made one last attempt. After several phone calls were made, I did find some third and fourth cousins who were descendants of Robert, brother of my John McMichael Boice. They were able to provide some current genealogy, but knew nothing about William.

And, that was it! William was not buried with Priscilla in the Union Presbyterian Church cemetery in Robinson Twp., Allegheny County. There was no will or estate inventory. Nothing made any sense. There seemed to be only one resolution to this mystery. I decided that William had died at a young age, and Priscilla dug a hole behind the barn and in he went.

The whole situation had become a real embarrassment. I was the editor of the *Boyce-Boice Bugle*, a quarterly newspaper and had announced to all that I would be compiling and writing a book entitled *Some Boyce-Boice Families - More Than 300 Years*. I was successfully researching quite a few Boyce-Boice lines, yet I wasn't able to do my own.

So, on that autumn day in 1989, I marched into my living room, faced the grouping of ancestral photographs on the wall and proclaimed out loud:

'John McMichael Boice, you must know something about your father, William. You must know something about your Boice grandparents. I've done everything I can possibly do. I need help!'

I continued this bizarre practice at least two or three times a week on into the spring of 1990. My four daughters and

The famous picture: John McMichael Boice.

older grandchildren agreed that I had 'gone off the deep end,' and that I should give up genealogy and return to the theater, which was more in keeping with my behavior.

My phone rang on 26 August 1990. The voice said that he was Benjamin R. Boice, M.D. of Idaho and the British West Indies. He had been on his way to visit his son in Maryland and had decided to stop at Burgettstown. Ben's grandfather had worked on family history for many years before and had determined that the family had roots in or near Burgettstown. After checking some cemeteries with no luck, Ben paid a call at the newspaper office of the *Burgettstown Enterprise*, made some inquiries and left his name and Idaho address. Eager to make a family connection, he then called one of the few Boices in the Pittsburgh area telephone directory. He reached one of my newly-found cousins, who directed Ben to me. We talked for some time. He said that his ancestor, John Boice (1785-1852) had brothers named William, Ebenezer, and Benjamin, and that they were the sons of John Boice (b. 1758 in Va.) and Margaret Allison. I was jumping with joy! We promised to exchange family information, and we did. In mid-September, Ben wrote that he had another family contact.

On 28 August 1990, just two days after Ben's visit, Wilma Rudkin Boice, wife of Frank (a descendant of Ebenezer), arrived in Burgettstown. She had traveled from Annapolis, Maryland. It was 9:30 a.m. and the town seemed to be deserted, except for some stirrings in the small office of the *Enterprise*. Wilma knocked at the door and asked the woman who responded if she could direct her to some early cemeteries: that she was working on her family history. 'How strange,' the woman said. 'Nobody comes *here* for genealogy information and just two days ago a couple from Idaho stopped by.' 'I think their name was Boice.' Wilma's chin hit her chest. She had not mentioned that *her* name was Boice. The woman gave her Ben's name and address.

Wilma wrote to Ben. Ben wrote to Wilma and me. I telephoned Wilma. It was an exciting time. During the course of our phone conversation, she casually mentioned that ten months earlier (the fall of 1989), she and Frank had attended a Naval Academy football game and an after-party, hosted by a neighbor. At that gathering, Wilma met Madelene McWilliams, who indicated that her mother was also a Boice and that they should get together sometime. They hadn't. Since I was researching *all human beings* named Boyce or Boice, I encouraged Wilma to call her - which she did. Information flew back and forth between Annapolis and Pittsburgh.

Madelene was a descendant of William Holmes Boyce (sometimes Boice), born 26 March 1797 in Washington Co., Pennsylvania. He served in the War of 1812. She thought that he may have had a previous marriage with sons named John and Robert. William had married Esther Strasser on 24 November 1831 in Stark County, Ohio and had moved frequently throughout the state. He died 22 October 1865 in Jackson County. They had seven sons named William, Benjamin, Frederick, James, Samuel, Daniel, and Ebenezer.

*Her William was my William.* What a scoundrel!! Poor, poor Priscilla. She lived for 30 years after William took off for Ohio. Maybe she should have dug that hole.

When the dust had settled, I approached the wall of photos.

'John McMichael Boice. I'm here again. I'm not sure how you made all of those strange events occur, but I do thank you. And, Great-Great-Grandfather, when you are rested, I have a few more holes to fill.'

I think he winked."

Going right to the source and talking to a deceased ancestor also seems to work for Jan Worthington of Australia. She writes,

"When we get frustrated with a particular job that appears to be getting nowhere, and our searches have been unproductive, my assistant Trish Thomson and I have been known to speak to one of our respective deceased parents. We get immediate results!"

But sometimes the results are not what we expect. An officer in the Marin County, California Genealogical Society related her tale to me. She had spent years looking for the ancestry of one of her grandparents, but to no avail. In desperation, she drove to the cemetery where her forebear was buried. It was a gray and overcast day, and the heavy clouds seemed to make the scene all the more dismal. She approached her ancestor's stone and made a long and eloquent plea for insight and revelation as to where to look for information on his parents.

Suddenly, as if in answer to her request, the clouds parted in the sky and a beam of light shone down on the old marker. Then a beautiful, snow-white bird descended from the sky, flew several times over the cemetery, and finally landed right on her grandfather's tombstone. The lady was overwhelmed at this sign from heaven, thinking that her prayer had been answered. And then, just when she thought that her life-long search was about to come to an end, the beautiful bird promptly lifted his tail, "decorated" the tombstone, and flew away.

OH, WELL, ... BACK TO THE LIBRARY!

## 16
## *REINCARNATION & LIFE ITSELF*

"I sometimes feel that I belong more in another century than in my own!" This was one of the most common feelings expressed by many of my genealogical colleagues in response to my query. And, as I've said before, that unsettling sensation is no stranger to me either. The Palatines haunt me! How often I've wished I was back with my 18th-century immigrants rather than dealing with the stress and strain of modern 20th-century life. My teenage daughter Amanda loves to give me the needle about this, teasing me by asking, "Ok, Dad, you know all about these old dead Germans: now tell me what color is the wallpaper in our bathroom?" I'm afraid I always "flunk" the test!

Some family historians believe that the concept of reincarnation might hold an answer to these uncanny inner stirrings. Evelyn S. Wache writes:

"I, too, feel that many of the experiences of our lives just don't idly happen. Whether they are part of the 'collective unconscious' or even due to past lives. I have read several books on reincarnation, and am quite openminded about the subject. I think all these possibilities should be studied and discussed."

And Christine Rose, as mentioned earlier, has told of her interest in the Edgar Cayce series of writings on reincarnation, and how she is fascinated by the whole subject.

I too am very open to the idea, especially considering my thirty-year obsession with all the 18th-century Palatine immigrants. The possibility that I once lived among them in their time frame certainly could explain a lot of the bewildering experiences that have occurred as I climbed the family tree: My likes and dislikes for certain Palatines - even though they've been dead for centuries. My sense of geographic déjà vu (when I knew what was around the next bend of the road on my first visit to the locales where the immigrants had lived - even though I'd never been there before). And that strange inner voice telling me, in no uncertain terms, to drop all other genealogical investigations and concentrate solely on this obscure group of dead Germans.

I have had many psychic "readings" given by reputable and distinguished mediums since that profound first experience at the Southern California Society for Psychical Research in 1979. Interestingly enough, each and every psychic, from Shama Smith to Jim Diehl to Freda Fell to the renowned Sylvia Browne, has told me that my sense of mission to tell the Palatines' story is simply the desire to complete a task started in another lifetime. I *knew* these people. I was one of them! What a fascinating concept!

I've discovered that reincarnation - where we all have many lives in which to learn our lessons, find our truths, and "get it right" - is not as foreign to western thought as one might think. In sharp contrast to many of their descendants, I learned the early Christians *did* believe in reincarnation, as had the Buddhists and Hindus for many centuries before the birth of Christ. References to it were found in earlier versions of both the Old and New Testaments but were deleted by the Roman emperor Constantine the Great at the Council of Nicaea in 325 A.D. In 553 A.D. the Second Council of Constantinople confirmed this act (probably fearing that reincarnation would weaken the church's power by giving members too much time to seek their salvation). So the idea of reincarnation *was* in my psychic roots after all: I just didn't know it! And far greater minds than mine have believed in it: men as varied as Napoleon, Benjamin Franklin, and Henry Ford. Good company!

Scientific research in the field is thriving. For example, Dr. Brian L. Weiss in his *Many Lives, Many Masters* writes a riveting story of his own and others' experiences in past-life-regression therapy. He notes the pioneering work of scholars such as Dr. Ian Stevenson of the University of Virginia. Dr. Stevenson collected over two thousand examples of children with reincarnation-type memories in his study. These youngsters had never been exposed previously to this concept and really were much too young to comprehend it if they had. But many exhibited xenoglossy, the ability to speak a foreign language to which they were never exposed, and possessed verifiable knowledge of events or locales for which there was no rational explanation.

Lately, I've been reading several scholarly studies of *group* reincarnation. For example, Arthur Guirdham's *We Are One Another* is an excellent analysis of eight people who lived and suffered as mediaeval Cathar heretics and then seem to have reassembled to live in the twentieth century in the same area of England. This whole subject is intriguing to me, because many times when first meeting a Palatine descendant, I've had the unexplainable feeling that I've known them somewhere before. It's as if we've been separated, but finally reunited again. Indeed, I have an unusual problem with a particular learned colleague of mine. He's been a dear friend now for over twenty years, a preeminent historian of the 1709er German immigrants. We can almost talk in a mental and verbal shorthand, so attuned to the Palatines and each other are we. But, hard as I try, *I cannot remember his appearance.* Whenever I think of him, I see *another* face in my mind, far different from his own. I can't help but wonder if I'm remembering a face I knew three hundred years ago?

In trying to learn more about soul survival (which ties in to all of this), I especially have enjoyed reading the pioneering studies of Dr. Raymond Moody, Dr. Elisabeth Kübler Ross, and many others detailing "near-death-experiences." The commonality of events related by individuals who have been clinically dead and then revived certainly is thought-provoking. So many of these people remember a sense of being dead, peace and painlessness even during a "painful" experience, bodily separation, entering a dark region or tunnel, rising rapidly into the heavens, meeting deceased friends and relatives who are bathed in light, encountering a Supreme Being/White   Light, reviewing one's life, and feeling reluctance to return to the world of the living. This lovely experience and memory can happen to all, no matter what their age, sex, status, ethnicity, or theological bent. And there is so much more well-documented literature on the subject just waiting to be examined. {If you really want a "good read" some night, ponder Sir William Barrett's 1926 classic *Death-Bed Visions: The Psychical Experiences of the Dying*:  that'll get you thinking!}.

Oh, what a fascinating area this all is! On the scientific front, even time itself is no longer necessarily a constant. Building on Einstein's curved space theory, physicists and astronomers are investigating anti-matter, and the possibility that a galaxy consisting of anti-matter time would permanently flow backward relative to ours. And Adrian Dobbs, working with quantum theory, has introduced a universal model in which *two* time dimensions exist instead of one, where precognition (the anticipation of future events) follows the second time dimension. Even the science-fiction concept of time-tunnels, which would permit direct contact between regions separated in normal space by astronomical distances, is being seriously studied to shorten the length of future space flights. Wow!

Jane Fletcher Fiske also is interested in this whole cosmic exploration. She writes,

"I believe that we're living in only one limited dimension of what is a limitless, very interesting, and ultimately good and loving universe. Every now and again we get glimpses of another dimension, but because these can't be scientifically measured, our more left-brained friends are afraid of what they can't understand and/or control. I think that changing, growing, and becoming more is what it's all about."

How I agree! When Jane penned a postscript to her letter, adding,

"Hank, my whole life feels like a testament to the other dimensions, but this isn't something I can discuss with most people" -

I felt I was in the presence of a true kindred spirit.

Sometimes we genealogists get awfully persnickety, territorial, and adamant in setting forth what we believe to be a correct family line. The old "I'm right, and you're not!" syndrome thrives. So feuds and bitter quarrels, unfortunately, are no strangers to the family history field. One of the most wonderful and rewarding side-benefits in tracing my psychic roots has been what I've learned from my colleagues - not just about genealogy, but about life! For instance, Jane Fiske's view of the good and loving universe seeps over into her daily work as editor of the prestigious *New England Historical & Genealogical Register*. In a recent book review, she talked about the wasted energy caused by a recent, vitriolic genealogical quarrel by reminding us:

"Genealogy is, basically, the study of people who are no longer living by people who are - and it is the latter group who necessarily bear the burden, and face the challenge, of making it a field worthy of respect. A holier-than-thou approach by experts striving for super-scholarship may earn the admiration of a few, but will do little but antagonize others. It does, moreover, encourage the kind of divisive ego-competition that grows into controversies which frequently outlive the participants.

The far-sighted pleasure that we as genealogists derive from accurately reconstructing the shadowy lives of our ancestors should not be allowed to obscure our nearer vision of those who share our own time and space. An individual who denies his or her responsibility to interact constructively with other human beings makes a mockery of what this study is all about - if people are not important, our fascination with our ancestors might more logically be directed towards fossils or postage stamps.

We suggest a saner attitude in which the sensitivities of the living are given better balance with the need for accuracy about the dead."

That review really got to me, showing again how genealogy can impact and affect us. Why sometimes climbing the family tree can change our entire life. Just ask Gordon Remington of Salt Lake City, Utah, who contributed a moving personal testament to the power of genealogy:

"Anyone who has been to Utah to conduct genealogical research is aware of the heightened religious atmosphere here. Over the thirteen years I have lived in Salt Lake City, I have heard many different stories of all sorts of 'genealogical miracles.' These stories range from very sincere people praying to find their ancestors and then a book falling off the shelf and opening to just the right page - to the woman with the divining rod who challenged the conclusions of a professional genealogist by pointing it at names on a pedigree chart. I was always skeptical of such stories, for as a professional genealogist I could not justify such an unscientific approach to my research. Nevertheless, I do have my spiritual side, which my professional colleagues seldom see overtly expressed.

In early 1989, I requested release from membership in the Salt Lake Monthly Meeting of the Society of Friends. This was quite a serious step, for I was a convinced Quaker - I had chosen Quakerism as a spiritual path shortly after my arrival in Salt Lake City, and had become a member of this Meeting in early 1984. For over eight months, I did not attend meeting. In retrospect, I can truly say that my heart had been hardened.

I eventually agreed to a clearness committee - a meeting of several Quakers who would listen to my grievances and give me counsel - but even it did not satisfactorily resolve my problems with the Meeting. I believe, however, that it did open the way to new insights and awareness.

Shortly thereafter, I was researching an Ellis family for a client. I had the surname Ellis in my own ancestry - but it being such a common name I did not think that there was any connection to the family on which I was working professionally, which was resident in Virginia in the mid-eighteenth century. My third great-grandfather, Joseph Ellis, was born in Maryland in the early 1820's and was married in Frederick County in 1845. He was an engineer on the Baltimore and Ohio Railroad who eventually settled in Newburg, Preston County, West Virginia. Not much was known about him by the family, except a vague tradition that he was of Welsh ancestry.

My own research into Joseph Ellis was conducted first at the Family History Library and then on-site in Preston County, West Virginia. By 1989 I knew that Joseph Ellis was born in July of 1824, and that his middle initial was 'R.' One census indicated that his father was from New Jersey, and another source suggested that his father's name was Daniel Ellis. Five years after Joseph's first wife Henrietta died in 1892, he sold his farm to one of his sons on the condition that he be allowed to live on it. His son reneged (Joseph was apparently too difficult to live with), and Joseph had to sue him in 1903 to get the land back.

Joseph married (at the age of 74) in 1898 to Myrtle Victoria Pyles, the 19 year old daughter of his tenant farmer John Pyles. Myrtle bore Joseph two more children - Rufus in 1899 and Milford in 1906 - and she bore *with* Joseph for almost ten years before she sued him for divorce. In her petition to the Preston County Circuit Court in 1908, she stated that Joseph was an abusive individual who beat her, accused her of infidelity, and did not provide financially for his family.

Interestingly, the divorce suit was dropped in 1910. Myrtle may have realized that her 86 year old husband did not have long to live, and that she stood to gain something from his estate. She was appointed his administratrix on 31 January 1913. Within the year, she had married a man ten years her junior and moved to Columbus, Ohio.

While I was pleased with myself for having found this information, I was really no closer to determining Joseph Ellis's parentage and ancestry. He was the first real 'black sheep' I had found in my own ancestry, and this possibly explains why not much had been passed down about him.

Which brings us back to that day in August of 1989 when I was searching that other Ellis line. As part of my general survey of Ellis literature, I came across an Ellis family in New Jersey that used the name Daniel. While I thought that this was probably just a coincidence, it led me to stop my client clock and look a little bit further into my own Ellis ancestry. The first exciting find was the christening record of Joseph *Ridgeway* Ellis, son of Daniel and Catharine Ellis, born *7 July 1825*, in a card index to miscellaneous records in Frederick County, Maryland. I had looked at this source many years before but had not found this entry, possibly due to the fact that Joseph's name only appeared on a card under the name of his father. The original church records showed that his date of birth was actually *7 July 1824* - an exact match to the month and year of birth as given in the 1900 census.

Joseph had a brother named Daniel 'Pleomus' Ellis. The name 'Pleomus' intrigued me, and Joseph's middle name - Ridgeway - led me to check *Ridgways in the U.S.A.* In this book I found that a Joseph Ellis, son of John and Lucia (*Ridgway*) Ellis, had married Rachel *Polhemus* in Burlington County, New Jersey in the late eighteenth century. Further research indicated that they had moved to Frederick County, Maryland. As I continued with the research, it became apparent that Daniel Ellis was the son of Joseph and Rachel (Polhemus) Ellis, and that he gave ancestral surnames to his sons as middle names.

In the next hours, I traced several of the lines suggested by this ancestry. The Polhemus and Ridgway lines led me into early Dutch and Quaker families in New Jersey. It seemed ironic that behind Joseph Ellis, a man of questionable character, there was a wonderful panorama of early Quaker ancestors. It was on the Ellis line that I made the discovery which means the most to me. Francis Ellis, the earliest ancestor in that family line, had married a first cousin of John Woolman. When I found this, my heart was pounding, and my hands were shaking. Given my spiritual condition at the time, it was significant for me to find this distant relationship to John Woolman.

Of all the Quaker worthies whom I had studied, I felt a particular affinity with John Woolman. He was the Quaker mainly responsible for the abolishment of slavery in the Society of Friends almost seventy five years before the Civil War. He is held in high esteem by many Quakers because of this. But my feelings for John Woolman ran deeper than what he was famous for, for I have no aspirations to try to do what he did.

John Woolman was a small businessman, a tailor, who earnestly tried to apply his religious principles to the manner in which he ran his business. As a small businessman myself, I looked to John Woolman as an example. He also left a journal, which has been published many times. Quaker journals are spiritual testimonies, designed to instruct and inspire the reader. The fact that John Woolman could also admit to his errors and the lessons he learned from them made him human - not some distant and perfect religious figurehead.

John Woolman's account of his early life mentioned experiences to which I could relate. When he was a child, he had thrown a stone at a bird and killed it, not knowing it was a mother with chicks to feed. Feeling remorse at what he had done, he killed the chicks so they would not suffer. When I was a teenager, I had fired a pellet rifle, for no good reason, at a rabbit. The rabbit ran away, and I followed it into a thicket. I had only wounded the rabbit, and the sight of it lying there, a victim to my senseless violence, made me ill. I honestly don't remember if I, like John Woolman, put it out of its misery.

Woolman also admitted that, as a teenager, he 'began to love wanton company,' and that 'youthful vanities and diversions were {his} greatest pleasure' - experiences and sentiments to which I could also relate. During my period of separation from the Meeting, I had returned to some of the bad habits of my youth. Through a series of chance meetings that afternoon and in the subsequent week, I was led to return to the Meeting and to give up these vices.

Finding John Woolman was a distant relative created a spiritual revival in me. I certainly did not think that I was a better person because of this relationship by blood - what this new relationship with John Woolman did for me was to remind me, at a time when I needed it most, of my old relationship with him and what it meant to me. Much in my life has changed for the better since that time, quickly in some aspects, slowly in others. Moreover, I had previously been obsessed with keeping my spiritual life separate from my professional life. As a result of this combination of circumstances, my life is much more in harmony.

I mark from that time a new beginning, and when I think back on it I wonder if it is just coincidence, as my rational, professional self tells me, or if there was something more to it. Why did it take almost ten years to find the answer and why did it happen at the time when it did - the time when I needed it most? Was it simply my inexperience at the time I originally searched that card index?

In Quakerism we have a phrase 'the way will open.'

Whatever the reason, a series of coincidences or something of deeper significance, the way did open for me. I may not be completely convinced that there was some greater force at work, but I do know one thing - when someone tells me a story like this one, I no longer laugh."

I no longer laugh either, Gordon! I have come to believe that we're being led on our searches, and so do many of our colleagues.

# 17
## BEING LED

Dr. David Faux of Hagersville, Ontario, has done extraordinary work in tracing his Palatine lines. After years of correspondence, we finally met in 1991 when I gave a series of speeches at the national Palatines To America conference in Cobleskill, New York. David observes:

"On a number of occasions during your talks, you alluded to the almost mystical quality of certain finds - as if some unseen hand was guiding you towards a target. This has, of course, happened to me, as it has to all of us genealogist types, a number of times. Perhaps you might be interested in the most dramatic of these.

A few years ago, I became a student of the military since I found that a large number of my ancestors had served in military campaigns across the whole globe. I was particularly intrigued by my grandfather's grandfather, Sgt. Charles Faux, who spent most of his life in India serving Queen Victoria. I followed his trail across India, including his marriage to a woman thirteen years his junior, and the births and burials of a number of little Fauxes in villages across India and Pakistan. He earned three medals, took his discharge in 1856, and returned to Norwich, England.

I had always dreamed of finding a picture of him, in uniform, and with his family. Realizing that the likelihood of this happening was infinitesimally small (he was only a sergeant), I was not deterred in the slightest - and made the location of such a portrait a major aim of my visit to England in 1986. I even had a picture in mind, and thought that I might have it photographed so I could display it in my living room. Dream on, David!

*The painting*

Courtesy Norfolk Museums Service (Norwich Castle Museum)

When I arrived in Norwich, I went to the local library and archives, and to the regimental museum - no luck. Towards the end of my visit (which included very fruitful trips to churches to see parish registers), I decided to do a bit of sightseeing. One major attraction in Norwich is the Norman castle in the centre of the city. It is also a museum and art gallery. After viewing the archaeological collections and the artifacts such as medieval armour, I had to occupy myself while a friend (a cat lover) went to see a particularly noteworthy collection of ceramic cats. Not seeing the need to spend inordinate lengths of time looking at cat figurines, I used the time to wander through a set of rooms housing the paintings of the Norwich School of Art. Upon entering one room, I stopped dead in my tracks as shivers ran down my spine!

I noticed immediately that across the room my grandfather's image was staring at me. The resemblance was astounding. As I approached the huge oil painting, I noticed that the man was in a British military uniform, with three stripes on his sleeve, and three medals on his chest. Not only that, but he was reclining on the bank of the local river in Norwich with a woman much younger than himself, and a child about three years of age. The artist was named Frederick Sandys, and the year of the painting was 1860. In 1860, my great grandfather was three years old, and living in Norwich with his young mother and much older father (who was then a sergeant in the Norfolk militia). The sitters for the painting were not identified, and I subsequently learned that the painter Sandys' papers appear not to have survived. However, I was able to learn that Sandys' father (with whom he stayed when coming from London) lived just around the corner from Charles Faux's residence. Also the medals depicted in the painting were the precise same three medals that Sgt. Faux earned in India.

I submitted my subsequent study of the painting to the two repositories where contemporary copies of the painting exist. Both curators told me that they are convinced beyond any reasonable doubt that the sitters were Sgt. Faux and his family. However, there is more to the story.

Before leaving the castle, I wanted to make arrangements to have the work copied. The person I spoke with said that it would not be necessary, as postcards and a large print suitable for framing were available for purchase in the gift shop! The print now occupies a very conspicuous place on our living room wall, and the postcards are in my family album.

Was I drawn to that room in the castle by some ethereal force determined that I should encounter the painting? It is almost as if the work was created just for me - so perfect a match was it to my original fantasy; and so unlikely was it that any such portrait should exist. As a scientist, I have a lot of trouble with paranormal explanations of phenomena - however, the whole business is exceedingly curious!"

Helen F. M. Leary of Raleigh, North Carolina, a guiding light and vital force in many genealogical organizations, is one of the field's most respected practitioners. She reflects:

"There is a very fine line between extended research by a person who already 'knows the territory' and the kind of twilight-zone communication that leads to an unexpected find in the 'wrong' place. These little flashes of unexpectedness happen to me so often, I was hard put to send you a specific example that could be analyzed for a distinction between the two phenomena. But I've just been in the twilight-zone again (I think), and here's what happened.

While doing a forty-hour search for a client's flit-about ancestor, the kind who seems determined to keep his identity secret, I had come about midway in the research and had begun compiling my findings for the report (this helps me direct the rest of the research). I'd done a lot of searching among the neighbors and the presumed collateral and related kin. One of the names was a compound one - like 'Whitewood' (which is not the name, but I'll use it as an example to preserve the client's anonymity). In the report, I felt I needed to explain why I was searching for 'Wood' as well as 'Whitewood' and so I inserted into the report a paragraph about the tendency of North Carolina clerks to abbreviate a compound surname by reducing the first 'word' to an initial - which has led to indexing and alphabetizing by the second word. Thus, 'John Whitewood' becomes 'John

W Wood.' One of the examples of this tendency that I chose for the report was 'Charles Chaneywolf,' who is occasionally found as 'Charles C Wolf.' Charles lived in one of the coastal counties I was investigating, which is probably what brought him to mind. He is not an example I usually use ('Seth Pettypoole/P. Poole' and 'John Broadhurst/B. Hurst' are my frequently-used examples). I had not encountered Charles among the elusive ancestor's neighbors and associates, however, and have never worked directly on his lineage.

I had found record of a man with the same name as the elusive ancestor witnessing a Granville District 'grant' for land in western North Carolina that was written while the land was in one county but filed after a new county was erected in the area. I needed to find out whether the document was signed at the courthouse in the old county, at the Granville land office, or out on the frontier where the land was located, so I undertook a survey of all the rest of the Granville grants issued on the same day (25 March 1752). I hoped to identify a pattern that would resolve the question. There were 88 grants of that date. The majority were incoming 'Scotch-Irish' and Germans from Pennsylvania and the Valley of Virginia; a few were to prominent land speculators who lived in eastern North Carolina (my man was in the 150-acre class). Twelve of the grants were not witnessed at all; the witnesses for all but two of the rest came from a five-man pool of Granville witnesses of the period. One of the two exceptions was the document of my initial interest. The other was issued to Johannes Gerhard, witnessed by Charles Robinson and John Bernhard Shoennewolff. Both grants were obviously signed out on the frontier, which is not where the elusive ancestor should have been in 1752 (the old-county courthouse was where I'd hoped to find him).

Abandoning what I believed had been an unproductive search, I continued tracking various clues with equally depressing results. In the last hour remaining of client's time, I returned to the records of the coastal county to re-check my initial notes, verify dates and name spellings, and all that sort of thing. I found that I had omitted the date in an excerpt of one court-minute entry. It was of minor significance, but in the interest of 'doing the work thoroughly,' I re-examined the minute book and leafed through the pages that preceded that entry to locate the date of the court session. Three pages before that entry, this is what I found:

> *'A Deed of Gift from John Barnard Shenawolf to his son Charles Shenawolf was acknowledged by the sd John Bernard and ordd. to be Recorded.'*

The court date was March, 1744. John Bernard also made a deed of gift to William Bush (probably his son-in-law), which was registered the same day, and, like the elusive ancestor, disappears from the records of coastal North Carolina (I tracked him for another of those unbillable hours we professionals are not supposed to have). As I said, I had never worked directly on Charles and had been quite unaware that his father was also in North Carolina; Charles himself is prominent enough in the records to be a useful guide for analyzing stray lists and notes that have no other date or place, and this had been my only experience of him.

I don't know yet whether Schoennewolff of the frontier and Shenawolf of the coast will turn out to be the same man, or whether (if he is) his move coincided with the elusive ancestor's (or even whether the same-name man on the frontier will turn out to be the ancestor). Additional research will need to be done. But previous experience tells me that good old John Bernard is going to be the key that will unlock the puzzle.

Although it is certainly true that I would not have found this gentleman if I hadn't been poking around among the collateral kin's neighbors, and if I hadn't been persnickety enough to search for the court date for an insignificant piece of information. That much you can ascribe to the 'experienced researcher' theory. But why did Charles pop into my mind BEFORE I had found either of the Shenawolf entries? And what made me RECORD the other grant document exception - the German names were expected in that area and time period, and 'this and one other were signed...' would have been entirely sufficient. And why was the March 1744 court entry the ONLY ONE I hadn't gotten the date for the first time around (i.e., before

I'd done the land-grant analysis)? If my research hadn't followed the precise order it did follow, I would have missed this potential gold-plated link entirely. (And, of course, why had the clerk chosen to use the "Sh" variant on that particular day when he normally used one of the "Ch" variants; and why was the Gerhart grant the only other exception out of eighty-eight?) Although the records were waiting for someone to find, the way they were found was unusual (to say the least). And so, to the strains of the Twilight-zone theme song, I will leave you... Spookily..."

Helen added an intriguing "P.S." by relating another story:

"I was looking for the wife of a client's proven ancestor. Returning to the 'scene of the crime' so to speak - that is, the neighborhood where the ancestor had grown up - I began searching among his proven father's kinfolk, geographical neighbors, and records associates. Client and I both hoped I would find a wonderful will naming 'my beloved daughter Jane, wife of John ...' And, of course, I did not find such a marvel. Following the principle of telling the client how you have spent your time (i.e., reporting negative as well as positive results) I began to type up my research notes. In my abstract of one of the less-than-likely associates, I had written something like '.... and to my executor {money} to purchase for my youngest daughter {unmarried} a silver ____.' I hadn't been able to read the word. I went back to the record and checked, and rechecked, and then re-read it again. All I could come up with from the handwriting (which was poor) was that he'd provided money to buy the girl 'a silver *hand*.' I included this nugget in the report just because it was a colorful puzzle; as I recall, the testator hadn't even supplied the girl's given name.

But, as the client informed me breathlessly by phone a few days later, I had FOUND JOHN'S WIFE. Among the family artifacts, preserved and handed down because it was a curiosity, was a child-size, sterling silver hand, beautifully made and decorated. According to tradition (which was so bizarre the client had not included it in the 'given' data), the ancestress in question had been born without a right hand and throughout her life had used this one in its place.

Although I readily admit to be compulsive, I still don't

know what drove me to make an extra trip to the archives to capture that one missing word. Well, yes I do know, but that's the question before us, isn't it."

Helen's closing to her letter still echoes in my mind:

"There really IS something to this kind of "speaking" from ancestors - if the researcher is carefully and sincerely trying to find and reconstruct that forebear - they WILL help. But it can't be done by trying to force them to speak; and it can't be done if the researcher isn't paying attention to the subtle clues and almost-silent messages."

Donald L. Schiele of Pittsburgh, Pennsylvania, remembers the unusual chain of events which led to finding more about his Stevens-Puckey family connection. His cousin Tom found a civil war letter tucked away in the Puckey Family Bible signed "David W. Stevens." None of the family knew who he was, except that their great-grandmother Puckey was a Stevens. Mr. Schiele wrote to the Huntingdon County Historical Society, where the Puckeys lived, on the off-chance that they might have information on the elusive David W. Stevens. They responded with one newspaper extract on other members of the family, but did say they would pass his query on to someone in the Society who lived elsewhere. Soon, one of their Board Members called him, introduced himself as Roy Stevens, and proceeded to share with Mr. Schiele the documented results of his years of intensive searching on the family. Mr. Schiele remarks,

"I had an ongoing feeling that invisible forces were guiding this research, and that our combined investigations now will benefit future generations to come. Timing has been phenomenal. What made my cousin Tom, not genealogically inclined, think to look in that worn-out Bible? What fluke caused an aide at the Society to run into a faraway Board Member? What force had caused Roy to go backward to 1743 from the very point I had come forward to the present and then be able to merge the material? Who has really been in charge of this work?"

F. Edward Wright, editor of the *Maryland Genealogical Society Bulletin*, noted in a recent issue,

"Undoubtedly luck plays a part in our research. Call it fate, serendipity, or what you will - some of us think our deceased ancestors are *actively* involved in our research. It comes as sweet success to stumble across an ancient scrap of paper on which are recorded dates, places, events - and most precious, anecdotes of our family."

The publication then went on to detail three articles in which serendipitous experiences played an important part.

Mr. Wright's remarks sound similar to views expressed by Bette Butcher Topp of Spokane, Washington:

"I have always wondered why you can be browsing the stacks in the Salt Lake Library, take a book down, and it opens to your ancestor! Of course, I have always believed that our ancestors do help us in many ways, bless their hearts. Many of us believe that."

I have remarked on how often Fred Sisser III of New Jersey and I have been mentally attuned at precisely the same moments in time via our unplanned telephone calls to each other. This carries over into our correspondence also. On 19 November, 1990, Fred was in the middle of writing a long letter to me. I "happened" to choose this time to phone him, interrupting his task. After we talked on the telephone, he returned to his correspondence and wrote:

"Now, Hank, I bet you can't guess who just called me! The spirits of all these later-arriving Palatines are watching over us, making sure we get in touch just at the right moment - it's truly remarkable!!!"

He then signed his letter,

"The New Jersey End of German Telepathy."

And not only did the Palatines gently nudge me along on my searches and lead me: sometimes they seemed to come on even stronger. Pushing, shoving, cajoling and prodding me too - making darn sure I wouldn't let up until their story was told! They almost seem to take over.

For example, after over a decade of gathering material for my *The Palatine Families of New York - 1710*, it took me (pre-computer/word processor days) four full years to type my camera-ready manuscript for the two volumes. And, strange as it sounds, I must say that I have very little recollection of the time and trouble it took in actually typing the 1300-plus pages of those books: it's sort of a big blur in time to me. It was as if another force was in control, something or someone else doing all the arduous work. I was just a vehicle - a conduit - to get the material down on paper and in print.

Of course, it was my book; but, in a larger sense, it wasn't my book at all. I identified with the great French impressionist Henri Matisse who wrote that, in regard to his paintings, he felt he was "only the medium - a channel for another energy."

And how that energy does permeate genealogy! Helen S. Ullmann of Acton, Massachusetts, had an extraordinary experience. As an active member of her L.D.S. church, the occurrence had a special significance to her. In many ways, it reminds me of a similar  incident that happened to Christine and Seymour Rose related earlier in this book:

"Books With A Past" read the sign in front of the store in Concord, Massachusetts. I suggested to my ten year old daughter, Linda, that we go in and look for an encyclopedia we'd been trying to find for a long time.  When the store clerk said they didn't have one, I decided to browse through the shelves. To my amazement, I found *The Walcott Book*, a family history published in 1925. My grandmother had owned a book just like it.

As we opened the volume to find my mother's name, my eyes fell on a reference to her Aunt Sonia. 'Isn't it silly,' I remarked. 'They called her a lady of foreign birth. Didn't they want to say she was Russian?' I had loved my Aunt Sonia, the little I had seen of her. She was a jolly woman with a wonderful accent. Her gentle husband, Uncle Dana, was a linguist who had begun working as an estate manager after he had gone deaf.

We bought the book and brought it home. Later that evening, as our son was flipping through it, an idea came to me. 'I wonder who used to own this book?' I said suddenly. My son turned to the front of the volume. 'Dana L. Walcott,' he read.

His words electrified me. Was that Uncle Dana's signature? I decided to write to Long Island, New York for Aunt Sonia's and Uncle Dana's marriage record. Not only did I find Uncle Dana's signature, which was a perfect match with the one in the book, but I also eventually discovered much biographical material on these dear relatives. I even found that they had had a previously-unknown child who died at birth. I then was able to do the 'temple work' for Aunt Sonia and Uncle Dana and 'seal' the unnamed baby to her parents.

How had the book traveled across the country from California twenty years after Uncle Dana's death, to end up in a used-book store within five miles of my house? Was it just chance that I had walked into that store, or was the Spirit prompting me to do something? All I know is that when I represented Aunt Sonia in the sealing of that unnamed baby to her parents in the Washington Temple a few months later, I felt an intense burning in my bosom unlike anything I had ever experienced; I couldn't contain my tears. Surely that is why *The Walcott Book* had traveled across the country."

The noted Canadian specialist Brenda Dougall Merriman reflects:

"I'm beginning to think that many things in my life do not happen 'by chance' but are in some design, certainly not of my conscious making. One of my major hobbies is reading. I find myself especially enjoying novels of intrigue/suspense/mystery/detection (naturally, as a genealogist) and also novels of historically researched background (which also follows, as a genealogist). And I have been aware for years that these novels which I seem to choose at random from the bookstore or library, on impulse according to what's currently available in medieval who-dun-its or serial killer fabrications or psychological thrillers, so often contain some critical sub-theme or concept in them that is uncannily applicable to my own life at the time. Not only in *one* book, but the important thing I'm going through in my life, is either the dominant or hidden-then-revealed theme that *recurs* book after book, whether I choose suspense or historical or spy novel 'at random.'"

If indeed we are being led in our searches and even watched over in our lives, there's almost a playfulness about it all by whomever is doing the guiding. Alan Vaughan in his *Incredible Coincidence: The Baffling World of Synchronicity* relates many cases that, besides being mind-boggling, are downright hilarious and revealed with precise timing and wit. I love his story of the West German farmer's wife who lost her wedding ring forty years ago in a potato field; she found it recently in her kitchen - inside a potato grown in that very field! Then too, as Vaughan looked for cases with synchronicity involving numbers, he reported that the most-needed quality for that search was a sense of humor.

Ditto in genealogy, as evidenced by so many experiences related in this book. Sometimes even a funny thing will happen on the way *to* the library! Myrtle Stevens Hyde of Ogden, Utah, writes:

"The good fortune is mine, genealogically, to live only thirty-two miles from the Family History Library in Salt Lake City, and I visit the wonderful facility regularly. Usually plenty of thinking occupies the driving time, and only rarely do I listen to the radio during the trip. A banner experience occurred one day, though, after the radio seemed a possibly nice diversion.

I turned the knob and listened to the entire range of stations. Finding nothing of interest, I switched the OFF knob. Then I looked heavenward and said out loud, 'What I really would like to hear is Beethoven's Fifth.'

A few more uneventful miles registered on the speedometer when I tried the radio again. This time, incredibly, the immortal harmony of the Fifth Symphony of Beethoven greeted my ears. Astounded, I turned the volume up and enjoyed.

My customary route into Salt Lake City exits the freeway north of the city and follows the old highway. I moved to the proper lane for turning, elated with the enchanting strains from the radio. Soon, however, the scenery was different out the window than usual. I had taken the wrong exit, immediately before the desired one, and was headed toward the Salt Lake International

Airport. Disbelief. And then I smiled.

The angels, I concluded, decreed that because they arranged the broadcast of Beethoven's Fifth for me, I would travel a long route and listen to the *whole* selection. I did, and savored every measure. The melodious last notes faded just as I reached my usual parking area near the Family History Library.

I almost heard the angels laughing."

**ME TOO, MYRTLE!**

## 18

## FROM THE TRUNK TO THE OTHER SIDE

Well, dear reader, our journey into the "Twilight Zone of Genealogy" is almost ended. Our psychic basement trunk has been explored. We've joined minds and hearts, shared thoughts and experiences, and made the trip together. It's been a fascinating and thought-provoking passage for me, and I hope it was for you too.

We genealogists are known for weighing the preponderance of evidence when firm documentation is lacking. And I now believe the evidence is overwhelming that serendipitous and intuitive events do indeed influence our research. The quality and quantity of such "psychic" experiences so generously shared by my fellow family historians attest to this. To refute so many respected friends and colleagues speaking from the heart, telling their truth as they see it, would be impossible.

Happily, my initial question as to whether I was alone in all this was answered early on in this project. Strong and clear, the message came through: we're all in this together! My associates' massive reenforcement of the unusual occurrences that I too have experienced reminds me of two personalized auto license plates I once saw and never forgot:

"WE   R   1"

and

"I   AM   U."

So simple, so true.

But still, as the song says, "What's it all about, Alfie?"

That's for each of us to decide, I think. But I do believe that our ancestors have no wish to be forgotten: they *want* to be found! As so many of my associates have shown in their marvelous stories and experiences, if we are prepared, immerse ourselves in the lives and times of our forebears, and then allow ourselves to be led in our searches - all kinds of wonderful results can happen. And being open to the intuitive nudges and serendipitous events that occur along the way can only help but ensure a successful conclusion to many of our genealogical searches.

In seeking our psychic roots, we really have been tapping our inner resources in a search for who we are. And who we are and how we fit into the universal scheme of things is really the big question  ... a question that won't be answered completely until we make yet one more journey.

A few years ago, I wrote a song that pretty-much captures my thoughts and feelings on all this:

## THE OTHER SIDE
### Words & Music By Hank Jones, ASCAP©

Someday - We will know
Someday - We will go
Traveling - With the aid of some sweet spirit
as  our guide
We'll take a cosmic ride
And reach "The Other Side."

Someday - We'll be free
Someday - We will be
Greeting all the others who passed over
long ago
The part will join the whole
In the fellowship of souls.

Questions we've been wanting to ask
Answers to those questions!
Finally - all the phantoms we fear
The trouble and tears
The struggles and weight of our years
here on earth will be gone!

Someday - Time will cease
Someday - We'll find peace,
Beauty, and dimensions far beyond
our mortal dreams,
We'll see what's been unseen
All on "The Other Side!"
All on "The Other Side!"

# PROFESSIONAL CREDENTIAL ABBREVIATIONS
## OF CONTRIBUTORS

A.G.      Accredited Genealogist

C.A.L.S.      Certified American Lineage Specialist

C.G.      Certified Genealogist

C.G.I.      Certified Genealogical Instructor

C.G.L.      Certified Genealogical Lecturer

C.G.R.S.      Certified Genealogical Record Searcher

F.A.S.G.      Fellow of the American Society of Genealogists

F.N.G.S.      Fellow of the National Genealogical Society

F.S.A.G.      Fellow of the Society of Australian Genealogists

F.S.G.      Fellow of the Society of Genealogists (England)

F.U.G.A.      Fellow of the Utah Genealogical Association

# CONTRIBUTORS

**Dr. W. Cary Anderson** of Decatur, Arkansas
Author of numerous articles and books, incl.*The Ancestry & Descendants of John Shaver, 1745-1835, The Douthit Family in America, The Catt Family in America.* Currently working on the Thomas & Katz families, & early settlers of Vincennes.

**Judge John D. Austin**, C.G., F.A.S.G., of Queensbury, New York
Principal genealogist for the Stephen Hopkins family, Five Generations Project of the Society of Mayflower Descendants. Former editor of the *New England Historical & Genealogical Register.* Expert on families of Warren, Washington, and Saratoga Counties, N.Y., Lecturer.

**June B. Barekman** of Chicago, Illinois
Author of many genealogical books, incl. works on Barrickman, Anthis, Etchison, Hess, and Coker families. Officer in many genealogical, historical & patriotic societies. Chicago Genealogical Society *Newsletter* columnist; Expert on Illinois and Indiana families.

**William V. H. Barker** of Shelton, Connecticut
Author of genealogical books on upstate New York, incl. *Early Families of Montgomery Co., N.Y., Early Families of Herkimer Co., N.Y.,* & *Early Families of Schoharie Co., N.Y.* Specialist in computer science as related to genealogy.

**Stephen Samuel Barthel**, A.G., of West Jordan, Utah
European Correspondent for the Family History Library. Author of over a dozen family history books as well as *Gazetteer of Parish & Civil Jurisdictions in East & West Prussia.* A developer of the Library Catalog on compact disk, which is part of the FamilySearch program.

**Barbara Baxter** of Southern Pines, North Carolina
Diligently researching her Baxter family which came to Cleveland, Ohio from England in 1850. Also expert on her several New York Palatine lines.

**Carol Willsey Bell**, C.G., of Youngstown, Ohio
Librarian, lecturer, editor, and specialist in Ohio sources. Author of many books, incl. *Ohio Genealogical Guide, Ohio Wills & Estates to 1850, First Families of Ohio Official Roster, Ohio Guide to Genealogical Sources, Ohio Genealogical Periodical Index: A County Guide.*

**Mary McCampbell Bell**, C.A.L.S., C.G.L., of Arlington, Virginia
Lecturer and seminar instructor specializing in Virginia research and sources. Winner of the Award of Merit from the National Genealogical Society in 1988. Trustee of the Board for Certification of Genealogists.

**Raymond Martin Bell**, Ph.D., F.A.S.G., F.G.S.P., of Washington, Pennsylvania
Teacher and author of many books, including *The Ancestry of Richard Milhous Nixon, The Ancestry of Samuel Clemens, Mother Cumberland: Tracing Your Ancestors In Central Pennsylvania.* Specialist in Pennsylvania sources and research.

**William W. Berkman** of Colorado Springs, Colorado
Tracing his own Berkman surname, with its myriad of spelling variations. Active in Colorado genealogical groups.

**Ervin F. Bickley, Jr.** of New Canaan, Connecticut
Searching many families, including Bickley, Felton, Pastorius, Tull, Iams, Vance, Chant, Stull, Row, Stoneman, Davis, and Mitchell.

**Carl Boyer, 3rd** of Santa Clarita, California
Publisher, editor, lecturer, and author of many books, incl. the *Ship Passenger Lists* series: *National & New England 1600-1825; New York & New Jersey 1600-1825; the South 1538-1825; Pennsylvania & Delaware 1641-1825.*

**Edward Reimer Brandt**, A.G., of Minneapolis, Minnesota
Author of *The Ott Family on Two Continents, Brandt Roots 1605-1989, An Introduction to German-American Genealogy* (with others). Expert in Germanic genealogy.

**Brian G. C. Brooks**, F.S.G., Dip. F.H.S., of Hove, East Sussex, England
Former Chairman of the Executive Committee of the Society of Genealogists in London. Noted professional genealogist, interested especially in records of solicitors, notaries public and proctors, and also Anglo-Australian genealogy.

**Donald R. Brown** of Harrisburg, Pennsylvania
Supervisor of the Genealogical/Local History Dept. at the State Library of Pennsylvania for many years. Expert on postcards and how they can be a resource for family history.

**Annette Kunselman Burgert**, F.A.S.G., of Myerstown, Pennsylvania
Author of many books on Pennsylvania German immigrants and their origins, incl. the series *Eighteenth Century Emigrants from German-Speaking Lands* (Vol. I - *The Northern Kraichgau*; Vol. II - *The Western Palatinate*; Vol III - *Northern Alsace*) and *Westerwald To America*.

**Barbara Smith Buys**, B.A., M.A., C.A.L.S., of Fishkill, New York
Author of *Old Gravestones of Putnam County, New York* and many articles in newspapers and magazines. Specialist in Dutch, French Huguenot, and Palatine families of the Hudson Valley of New York.

**George F. Capes** of Rochester, New York
A longtime specialist in many New York families, many among them of Palatine extraction.

**Herlinda Taylor Carney** of Ventura, California
Active in several genealogical organizations on the west coast. Family historian of many groups, including her Bruce line.

**Jane Adams Clarke** of Philadelphia, Pennsylvania
Lecturer, editor, and author. Member of the Board of Directors of the Genealogical Society of Pennsylvania. Editor of its publication *Penn in Hand.* Contributor to many periodicals.

**John Insley Coddington**, F.A.S.G., F.S.G., F.N.G.S.
Late author of over 200 articles in leading genealogical periodicals. Contributing editor to *The American Genealogist*. First recipient of the New England Historical and Genealogical Society Award of Merit. Founding member of the American Society of Genealogists.

**Mary Ann Cole** of Kenosha, Wisconsin
Family genealogist of the Buxton, Trail, Northcraft, Sears, and Shinn surnames.

**Dorothy Craig** of Rancho Murieta, California
Family historian who writes that she keeps hoping for a book to fall off the library shelf and land open to tell her more about her great-great-grandparents Samuel G. Jackson (1821-1889) and Catherine Beauford Kirker (1827-1912) of Liberty Twp., Adams County, Ohio.

**Peter Stebbins Craig**, J.D., F.A.S.G. of Washington, D.C.
Historian and genealogist specializing in the study of the 17th-century immigrants to "New Sweden" on the Delaware River and their colonial descendants. Author of more than a dozen books and articles on the Swedish church censuses in that area and the families noted therein.

**Carol Boice Jones De Paul** of Pittsburgh, Pennsylvania
Author of a book in progress on the Boyce/Boice family, which includes the 17th-century Irish Quaker Boyes and Dutch Buijs surnames. Contributor to *Keyhole*, quarterly of the Genealogical Society of Southwestern Pennsylvania.

**Winston De Ville**, F.A.S.G., of Ville Platte, Louisiana
Publisher, and author/editor of some 34 genealogical reference works and over 100 articles. Specialist in families of the colonial Mississippi Valley and the Gulf Coast, incl. those of French and Spanish origin who settled the region in the 17th and 18th centuries.

**Paul I. Edic** of Akron, Ohio
Expert on families such as Ittig/Edick/Edic/Edee, Hofgut, Hocevar/Hochewar, Peek, Wellar/Weller, Mattausch, Bretterklieber, and Jones.

**Oran S. Emrich** of Kansas City, Missouri

Author of twelve books on the Emrick family, as well as studies of the Gingrich/Engel and Barnhart/Patterson families.

**Dr. David Faux**, C.G., of Hagersville, Ontario, Canada

A specialist in Ontario, Loyalist, and Six Nation Indian sources, with publications in all these areas. Interested in links between genealogy, military history, and archaeology. Expert in records of many countries, incl. England and India.

**Mary Smith Fay**, C.G. of Houston, Texas

Trustee for the Board of Certification of Genealogists, lecturer, active in many patriotic, historical, and genealogical groups. Author of several books, incl. *War of 1812 Veterans in Texas*, *The Hunsinger Family of White Co., Illinois*, *Edwin Fay of Vermont and Alabama*.

**P. William Filby**, F.N.G.S., F.U.G.A., F.S.G., of Savage, Maryland

Former Director of the Maryland Historical Society. Compiler of many books, incl. *Passenger & Immigration Lists Index, Bibliography of Ship Passenger Lists, American & British Genealogy & Heraldry, Who's Who in Genealogy*.

**Jane Fletcher Fiske**, F.A.S.G., of Boxford, Massachusetts

Editor of the *New England Historical & Genealogical Register*. Author of many articles and several books, incl.*Thomas Cooke of Rhode Island*. Specialist in 17th-century New England families and their English origins, and the settlers and court records of Rhode Island.

**Kenneth Frederick** of Lake Forest, Illinois

Author of *The Frederick Family of Rural Albany County, New York*, a record of the total descendants of the 1738 German Palatine emigrant Michel Friederichs. Expert in 25 early Dutch families who played key roles in the early history of Albany County, New York prior to 1664.

**Duncan B. Gardiner**, Ph.D., C.G., of Lakewood, Ohio

Specialist in research in Czechoslovakia, Yugoslavia, and Central Europe. Author of *The Antl and Schuerger Families of Metzensiefen,* and other family histories.

**John Terence Golden**, Ph.D., of Columbus, Ohio
Editor of *Palatine Immigrant*. Expert on the Irish, German, and French immigrants to the mid-western U.S.A.

**Dr. Bernd Gölzer** of Stiring-Wendel, France
One of Europe's most prominent genealogists. Author, lecturer. A specialist in German research and the families of Alsace.

**La Fay Eastman Gowan** of Hoover, Alabama
Author of *John Taner - A Florida Man,* and *Canada & Canaday Families of Florida & Georgia.* Working on many lines, incl. Shelby, Cobb, Gowan, Davis, Moore, Hart, Nettles, Cox, Walden, Cason, McDonald, Miller, Currie, and Eastman.

**Karen Mauer Green** of Galveston, Texas
Publisher, and author of many books, among them *The Kentucky Gazette: 1787 - 1820, Pioneer Ohio Newspapers: 1793 - 1818, The Maryland Gazette: 1727 - 1761.* Specialist in English, frontier Kentucky, and Northwest Territory research and sources.

**Charles M. Hansen**, F.A.S.G., of Sausalito, California
Author of *The Barons of Wodhull* and many articles on English Quaker immigrant origins, medieval genealogy, and heraldry. Has written extensively on the ancestry of King Charles II of England.

**Helen L. Harriss**, C.G., of Pittsburgh, Pennsylvania
Lecturer, educator, and specialist in Western Pennsylvania research. Author of many publications, incl. *Abstracts of Deed & Will Books of Allegheny Co., Pennsylvania.* Editor of *Jots From the Point,* newsletter of the Western Pennsylvania Genealogical Society.

**Faith G. Haungs** of Lockport, New York
Family genealogist with over 20 years experience. Hard at work on the soon-to-be-published *300 Years of the Haungs Family.* Also expert on all the families of St. Dionys Catholic Church, Moos, Baden, Germany.

**Anna Harvey** of Richmond, Vermont
Family genealogist with many U.S. and Canadian lines. Expert on some of the 1709er Palatine families such as the Bests, and also tracing later arrivals such as the Schneiders.

**Douglas Lindsay Haverly** of Loudonville, New York
Librarian and historian of the New York State Chapter of Palatines To America. Family genealogist tracing the Hoeflich-Haberle-Haverly family of Germany and New York.

**Dexter Hawn** of Ottawa, Ontario, Canada
Author of articles on Palatines and Loyalists. Expert on many families, incl. Hawn/Hahn, Rup(p)ert, Alguire, Servos, Schnäbelin, Shaver, Bush, Gallinger, Cryderman, Otto, Claus, Staring, Haus, Schwerdtfeger, Merckley, Broeffel, Ecker, Rickerd, and Huls.

**GeLee Corley Hendrix**, C.G., F.A.S.G., of Greenville, South Carolina
Author of many books, incl. *The Jury Lists of South Carolina 1778-79, Indexes of Edgefield Co., South Carolina Probate Records, Alexander Reid 1700-1777 and His Descendants*. Has written many articles in major publications. Specialist in problem-solving in "burned" counties.

**Marty Hiatt**, C.G.R.S.,of Lovettsville, Virginia
Active in the Association of Professional Genealogists. Conducts classes, seminars, and workshops on family history throughout the country.

**Helen Hinchliff**, Ph.D. of Fulford Harbour, British Columbia, Canada
A family historian who reconstructs the lives of genealogically-challenging 18th-century ancestors. Her paper on Michael Mumper, who emigrated from Germany to Pennsylvania in 1751, won first place in the 1988 NGS family history writing contest. Currently, she is writing a book on genealogical problem-solving, using her Scottish ancestors as case studies. Her academic degrees are in Political Science and Communications, and she is a graduate of three advanced courses in

genealogical, archival, and historical research. She is the author of numerous articles on genealogical research methods and sources.

**Maurice R. Hitt, Jr.**, C.G., of Binghamton, New York
Expert on Broome County, New York sources and families. Family historian for the Hitt family.

**David P. Hively** of Red Lion, Pennsylvania
Officer in the Pennsylvania Chapter of Palatines To America. Editor of the *Hively Family Newsletter.*

**Harry Hollingsworth**, C.G., of Inglewood, California
Expert on Irish genealogy. Author of several books, incl. *Records of the Parish of Arklow, County Wicklow, Ireland, Records of Crawford Co., Pennsylvania, Early Census Records of Venango Co., Pennsylvania.* Editor of *The Hollingsworth Register* since 1965.

**Myrtle Stevens Hyde**, F.A.S.G., of Ogden, Utah
A contributing editor to *The American Genealogist* and specialist in tracing the English origins of early New England families. Author of many articles and books, incl. the 3-volume *The Aldous Genealogy* and several in-depth studies of various Hyde-Hide families.

**Mary Jane Johns** of Oxnard, California
An active member and officer in several genealogical organizations, incl. the California State Genealogical Alliance. Family historian of her own lines, and her husband's Harrison, Hartshorn, Knight, and Clark families.

**Ken D. Johnson** of Grand Island, Nebraska
An expert on 18th-century families of the Mohawk Valley, New York. Historian tracing the lives and times of all who were involved in revolutionary war activities at Fort Plank in that region.

**Rick Kampf** of Vernon, British Columbia
Genealogist specializing several family lines in various regions, incl. Juelfs, Kampf, Borgerson, Turner, and Milligan.

**C. Frederick Kaufholz**, F.A.S.G., of Lakeville, Connecticut
Author of several books on Germanic genealogy, incl. *A Few Wuerttemburg Families of Grafenberg, Kohlberg, Riederich, & Tischardt, Die Familien Bauer und Theodald von Lachen-Speyerdorf* ... Specialist on the old families of Duderstadt, Germany.

**William C. Kiessel** of Bearsville, New York
Author and editor of innumerable books and articles. Contributor to the *New England Historical & Genealogical Register* and other national publications. Local historian of the Woodstock-Bearsville area in Ulster Co., New York.

**Helen F. M. Leary**, C.G., C.G.L., F.N.G.S., of Raleigh, North Carolina
President of the Board of Certification for Genealogists. Nationally-known lecturer on North Carolina research, general genealogical methodology in the southeast, English common law in the southern colonies, and professional genealogy practices. Author and teacher.

**Dale J. J. Leppard** of Carlisle, Pennsylvania
Longtime researcher of many family lines, incl. Finkenbinder, Leppard, Lehman, Zaccaria, di Mose, and Rieth.

**Lahoma Lindeman** of Layton, Utah
Researcher for 50 years, specializing in Cork County, Ireland, England, Ontario, the New England States, New Jersey, and Pennsylvania. Expert in deciphering the German churchbooks of the Rheinland and Hessen.

**Karen E. Livsey** of Falconer, New York
Librarian, and author of *Western New York Land Transactions* (Extracts from the archives of the Holland Land Company). Expert in the families and sources of western New York.

**Alice W. Long**, C.G.R.S., of Mt. Desert, Maine
Contributing editor to the *Maine Genealogical Society Journal*. Editor of *Vital Records of Mount Desert, Maine and Nearby Island 1776-1820, Marriage Records of Hancock County, Maine Prior to 1892*. Associate editor of *Maine Families in 1790, Vol. II*.

**Dorothy M. Lower**, C.A.L.S., of Fort Wayne, Indiana
Head of the historical and genealogical dept. of the Fort Wayne Library for many years. Author of *Bibliography of Basic Genealogical Sources, Passenger & Immigration List Index, The Patriots: Sketches of the Known Soldiers of the American Revolution Buried in Allen Co., Indiana.*

**Joan Lowrey** of La Jolla, California
President of the German Research Association. Specialist in Germanic sources and computer usage in genealogy. Author of *Personal Ancestral File 2.2 Users Guide, The Green Family: the Ancestors & Descendants of Barzilla Green.* Genealogical columnist.

**David Kendall Martin**, F.A.S.G., of West Chazy, New York
Author of many books, incl. *A History of the Town of Chazy, Chazy & the Revolution, La Corne St. Luc - His Flame,* plus genealogies of several 18th-century Mohawk & Hudson Valley, New York Palatine families such as Zimmermann, Failing, Snell, Kilts, and Clapper.

**John McCornack** of Peoria, Illinois
Author of over 20 genealogical books on various families. Coordinator for all information on the McCornack and McNatt families in America. Specialist on the families which lived in the Newton Stewart area of southwest Scotland in the early 1800s.

**Marie Varrelman Melchiori**, C.G.R.S., of Vienna, Virginia
One of the directors of the National Institute of Genealogical Research. Lecturer. Specialist in Civil War sources and research.

**Brenda Dougall Merriman**, C.G.R.S., C.G.L., of Guelph, Ontario, Canada
President of the Canadian Federation of Genealogical & Family History Societies. Author of many articles on research techniques, interpreting sources, & original source transcriptions. Books incl. *Genealogy in Ontario: Searching the Records.*

**Ejvor Merkley** of Mesa, Arizona
Co-author of *The Descendants of Christopher Friedrich Merckel (Merkley).* Expert on many Palatine families.

**Mary Keysor Meyer**, F.N.G.S., of Mt. Airy, Maryland
Former genealogical librarian at the Maryland Historical Society. Author of many books, incl. *Directory of Genealogical Societies in the U.S.A. & Canada, Genealogical Research in Maryland: A Guide, Passenger & Immigration Lists Index, Who's Who in Genealogy & Heraldry.*

**Joan Kirchman Mitchell**, Ph.D., of Tuscaloosa, Alabama
Lecturer and educator. President of the Tuscaloosa Genealogical Society. Editorial assistant for the *National Genealogical Society Quarterly.* Expert on the biological, medical, and psychological aspects of genealogy. Specialist in census records and their "hidden" data.

**George Moore** of White Stone, Virginia
Retired medical director of the U.S. Public Health Service. Author of several articles on his ancestry, including "Adam Hyler - Celebrated Privateer" in the *S.A.R. Magazine.* An expert in the German families of Hunterdon and Somerset Counties, New Jersey.

**Joy Wade Moulton**, C.G., F.S.G., of Columbus, Ohio
Lecturer, teacher, editor, and President of the Council of Genealogy Columnists. President of the International Society for British Genealogy & Family History. Author of *Genealogical Resources in English Repositories.*

**Marie Martin Murphy** of Bartlett, Illinois
Expert on the Martin family. Specialist in Kentucky and Shenandoah Valley, Virginia sources. Active in many organizations, incl. the Genealogical Speaker's Guild.

**Frederick T. Newbraugh** of Berkeley Springs, West Virginia
Lecturer and Columnist. Long-time researcher pursuing his family's ancestral lines.

**Nils William Olsson**, F.A.S.G., of Winter Park, Florida
Editor and publisher of *Swedish American Genealogist.* Author of many books, incl. *Tracing your Swedish Ancestry, Swedish Passenger Arrivals in New York 1820-1850, Swedish Passenger Arrivals in U.S. Ports 1820-1850 (excluding New York), Memoirs of Gustaf Unonius.*

**Gerald J. Parsons**, F.A.S.G., of Syracuse, New York
Formerly head genealogical librarian at Onondaga Co. Public Library. Contributing editor to *The American Genealogist*. Author of *The Parsons Family: Descendants of Cornet Joseph Parsons (1618-1683) ..., The Gorham Family: Ancestors & Descendants of Ephraim Gorham ...*

**Hazel C. Patrick** of Herkimer, New York
Expert on the Mohawk Valley, New York. Author of many books which detail the families of that region. The chief genealogist for the Herkimer County Historical Society.

**Dewayne E. Perry** of Summit, New Jersey
Genealogist of the Mell and Polley families, among many other groups.

**Mary A. Pitts** of Citrus Heights, California
Librarian for "Root Cellar" of the Sacramento Genealogical Society, Sacramento, California.

**Donna J. Porter**, C.G., of Denver, Colorado
Former President of the Colorado Genealogical Society and the Colorado Chapter of Palatines to America. Genealogical bookstore owner. Author of *Welding Link: an Introduction to Genealogy, Virginia Area Key: Genealogical Aids for the State of Virginia.*

**Elissa Scalise Powell** of Wexford, Pennsylvania
Author of articles on family history and serendipity in genealogy. Historian of several families, incl. Auble, Baughman, Bechtel, Eberhart, Effinger, Gindner, Aiello, Battinelli, Scalise, Fanoni, Regoli, Bowman, and Brown.

**David Putnam, Jr.**, A.G., of Salt Lake City, Utah
Correspondence specialist at the Family History Library in Salt Lake City. Instrumental in developing key research guides for the thirteen colonies and their records. Author of *The Life Story of John Andrew Kofoed (of Weston, Idaho).*

**Kathleen T. Rasmussen** of Mountain View, Wyoming
Expert on the several families, incl. Thayne (Scotland), Crocket (England & Wales), Falkner (Eschelbach, Germany), Lulay/Wohlgemuth (Heppenheim, Germany), Gough, Hales, & Brockbank (England).

**Roger K. Rasmussen** of Salem, Oregon
Expert on Fayette County, Pennsylvania families, incl. Field, Miller, Gaddis, Britt, Davis, Rowland, and West. Cemented his Danish roots and established ties with family members still in Europe. Hard at work on the Thrashers of Shelby County, Missouri and the Lansings.

**Gordon Lewis Remington**, F.U.G.A., of Salt Lake City, Utah
Has served as a board member of the Utah Genealogical Association and the Association of Professional Genealogists. Former editor of *The Genealogical Journal.* A frequent speaker at national and international genealogical conferences.

**Douglas Richardson** of Tucson, Arizona
Prolific author of many articles in major genealogical publications. Contributing editor to *The American Genealogist.* Author of *Eno & Enos Family in America.* Expert on the Amos Richardson family and the English origins of other colonial groups.

**Marsha Hoffman Rising**, C.G., C.G.L., F.A.S.G., of Springfield, Missouri
President of the Federation of Genealogical Societies, Trustee of the Association of Professional Genealogists, President of the Genealogical Speaker's Guild. Author of many articles on genealogical research and problem-solving.

**Doris Dockstader Rooney** of Dodge City, Kansas
Author of the three-volume *The Dockstader Family in America*, a study of one of the Mohawk Valley's most important Palatine families. A founder and active member of the Kansas Genealogical Society.

**Christine Rose**, C.G., C.G.L., F.A.S.G., of San Jose, California
Winner of the Donald Lines Jacobus Award for two of her books on the Rose family. A Director of the Federation of Genealogical Societies, Regional Vice-President of the Association of Professional Genealogists. Founder of the nationwide Rose Family Association.

**Eunice Ross** of Pittsburgh, Pennsylvania
Judge, Court of Common Pleas, Pittsburgh, Pennsylvania. Active researcher on her own Pennsylvania Swiss and German lines.

**Melinda Lutz Sanborn** of Derry, New Hampshire
Author of *Essex County, Massachusetts Probate Index: 1638 - 1840, Hayes & Allied Families of Glouster County, Massachusetts, Vital Records of Hampton, New Hampshire.*

**William B. Saxbe, Jr.**, C.G., of Oberlin, Ohio
Award-winning author of several books, incl. *Thomas Saxbe (1810-1860) and his Descendants, Landowners in Champaign Co., Ohio, 1874, Saxby Family Records in Buckingamshire, Johann Genning (1818-1898) and His Descendants: a Toledo Family.*

**Donald L. Schiele** of Pittsburgh, Pennsylvania
Tracing his mother's Puckey/Stevens lines and his father's German forebears. Active in the Western Pennsylvania Genealogical Society & the Cornwall Family History Society. Writes, "I have a growing belief that my honored ancestors are aware of and aiding the effort."

**James Owen Schuyler** of San Carlos, California
Active in tracing his many family lines here and abroad. Expert in the complex New York Schuyler family.

**Morris A. Shirts** of Cedar City, Utah
Family genealogist of the Schertz/Shirts family of Germany, New York, Utah, and New Jersey.

**Fred Sisser III** of Bridgewater, New Jersey
Specialist in families of New Jersey. Former editor of *Somerset County Genealogical Quarterly.* Author of several books, incl. *The Monfoort Family of New York & New Jersey.* Active member of many organizations, incl. the Hunterdon County Historical Society.

**Dyan Kaye Sparling** of Joshua Tree, California
Family genealogist of the Sparling family. Along with its allied lines, she has traced over 10,000 family members here and abroad.

**Malcolm H. Stern**, D.H.L., D.D., F.A.S.G., of New York, New York

Teacher, lecturer, and author of many books, incl. *Americans of Jewish Descent: Sources of Information, Americans of Jewish Descent: Compendium of Genealogy, First American Jewish Families: 600 Genealogies, The Function of Genealogy in American Jewish History.*

**Eugene A. Stratton**, F.A.S.G., of Manchester, New Hampshire

Contributing editor to *The American Genealogist.* Expert in the origins and American activities of colonial New England families. Author of *Plymouth Colony: its History & People 1620-1691, Applied Genealogy, Killing Cousins.*

**Kenn Stryker-Rodda**, C.G., F.N.Y.G.&B.S., F.N.G.S.

Late lecturer, teacher, editor, & author of many books, incl. *Long Island Genealogical Source Materials, Digging for Ancestors in the Garden State, Genealogical Research Methods & Sources, Denizations, Naturalizations, & Oaths of Allegiance in Colonial New York.*

**Neil D. Thompson**, Ph.D., C.G., F.A.S.G., F.S.G., of Salt Lake City, Utah

Editor of *The Genealogist.* Past President of the Board of Certification of Genealogists. Executive Director and Trustee of the Association for the Promotion of Scholarship in Genealogy, Ltd. Expert in colonial America, 16th- to 18th-century England, noble families of Europe.

**Bette Butcher Topp** of Spokane, Washington

Active officer in the Eastern Washington Genealogical Society. Author of several books, incl. *The Kiddoo Family in the U.S. 1780-1981, Alexander Agenda, Bush Branches, Carpenter Chronicles,* and *Stratton Notes.*

**Helen S. Ullmann**, C.G., of Acton, Massachusetts

Specialist in Norweigian research. Author of *Naugatuck, Connecticut Congregational Church Records 1781-1901, Index to the Vital Records of Acton, Massachusetts, Subject Index to the Connecticut Nutmegger.* Expert in all families of Asker and Baerum, Norway.

**Wallace Van Houten** of Middleburg, New York
Active officer in the New York Chapter of Palatines To America. Expert on the 1709er families of Neher, Lösch, Dygart, Fuchs, and Kopp.

**Nancy Vannoller** of Coopersville, Michigan
Genealogist specializing in many families, incl. Alcook (Alcock), Reiling, Noss, Hamilton, Munson, Sachette, Trowbridge, Barringer, Nagle, DeWitt, Stranahan, Harding, Card, Vannoller, Besaw, King, Doxtater, Carlson, Cool, and Dosch.

**Nick Vine Hall**, Dip. F.H.S. (Hons), F.S.A.G., of Albert Park, Australia
Former Director of the Society of Australian Genealogists. Trustee of the International Society for British Genealogy & Family History. Author of *Tracing Your Family History in Australia, Parish Registers in Australia*, and others. Broadcaster & genealogical talk-show host.

**Evelyn Smith Wache** of Palenville, New York
A direct descendant of two Palatine 1709ers, Johann Henrich Schmidt and Peter Oberbach, who settled in what now is Greene County, New York. The two lines came together in 1915 with the marriage of her parents, George W. Smith and Letitia Myrtle Overbaugh, at Palenville.

**Mark L. Wahlqvist**, M.D., Professor of Medicine, of Clayton, Australia
Active in tracing his many lines in Australia and Scandinavia. Specialist in emigrant materials and sources of three continents.

**David Jay Webber** of Harwich, Massachusetts
Expert on his New York Palatine lines. Specialist in colonial Lutheran history and sources.

**Maralyn A. Wellauer** of Milwaukee, Wisconsin
Lecturer. Editor of *The Swiss Connection*. Author of many books, incl. *A Guide to Foreign Genealogical Research, Tracing Your German Roots, Tracing Your Swiss Roots, Tracing Your Norwegian Roots, Tracing Your Polish Roots*. Expert on 19th-century Swiss immigrants to Wisconsin.

**Elizabeth Whitten** of Huntsville, Alabama

Author of *Livingston Lines, The McDaniel Book, Perry Pioneers, EngLedow Family Collections, A Whitten Family History - Vol. I & Vol. II.*

**Friedrich R. Wollmershäuser**, A.G., of Oberdischingen, Germany

Lecturer, bookseller, and author of many works, incl. *Aus der Enge in die Weite - Geschicte der Familie Dillenius, German Genealogical Documents of the 15th to 19th Centuries.* Actively indexing censuses of southwest Germany. Expert in emigration sources and research.

**Nell Sachse Woodard** of Oceanside, California

Lecturer, teacher, and author. Books incl. *Robert A. & Martha Meachem Thompson, Chamberlain, Wilson & Hunt, Ancestry's Red Book (Section on the West).*

**Jean D. Worden**, C.G.R.S., of Zephyrhills, Florida

Author of many churchbook transcriptions of the New York State area, incl. registers of New Hurley, Fishkill, Kingston, Montgomery, Shawangunk, and many others. Indexed the New York Genealogical & Biographical Society's *Record.*

**Janet Worthington**, Dip. F.H.S., of Sydney, Australia

Lecturer, and author of *Computers & Genealogy, Introduction to Genealogical Software, The Dalby Years.* Active in worldwide genealogical organizations, incl. the 1st International Congress on Family History.

**F. Edward Wright**, of Westminster, Maryland

Publisher, and author of many books, incl. *Maryland Militia, Caroline County Census for 1820 & 1860, Caroline County Newspaper Extracts, Maryland Militia in the Revolutionary War, Maryland Eastern Shore Vital Records, Vital Records of Kent & Sussex Counties, Delaware.*

**Franklin A. Zirkle** of Roanoke, Virginia

Author of *Brock Family of the Shenandoah Valley of Virginia,* and several articles incl. one published in *National Geographic Magazine.* Historian of the Zirkle, House, Rosenberger, Biedler, and Kagey families.

A sequel to *Psychic Roots* is being planned.

Readers of this book are invited to share their own serendipitous and intuitive genealogical experiences with the author and may contact him at the following address:

Henry Z Jones, Jr., F.A.S.G.
P. O. Box 261388
San Diego, California
92196-1388

# BIBLIOGRAPHY
## (& SOME GOOD BOOKS TO CURL UP WITH ON A RAINY NIGHT)

Barrett, Sir William. *Death-Bed Visions: The Psychical Experiences of the Dying.* (Wellingborough, UK: The Aquarian Press, 1986 from a 1926 work).

Brown, Sylvia, & May, Antoinette. *Adventures of a Psychic.* (New York: Signet Books, 1991).

Burgert, Annette K., & Jones, Jr., Henry Z. *Westerwald To America.* (Camden, Maine: Picton Press, 1989).

Campbell, Joseph, with Bill Moyers. *The Power of Myth.* (New York: Doubleday, 1988).

Cayce, Hugh Lynn, and Cayce, Edgar. *God's Other Door and the Continuity of Life.* (Virginia Beach: A.R.E. Press, 1958).

Guirdham, Arthur. *We Are One Another - A Record of Group Reincarnation.* (Wellingborough, Northamptonshire, UK: Turnstone Press Ltd., 1974).

Jones, Jr., Henry Z. *The Palatine Families of New York - 1710* (Universal City: 1985).

Jones, Jr., Henry Z. *More Palatine Families* (Universal City: 1991).

Jones, Jr., Henry Z. *The Palatine Families of Ireland* (Camden, Maine: Picton Press, 1990).

Jung, C. G., with Aniela Jaffe. *Memories, Dreams, Reflections.* (New York: Random House, 1965).

Jung, C .G. *The Portable Jung.* Edited by Joseph Campbell. (New York: The Viking Press, 1971).

Jung, C. G. *Synchronicity: An Acausal Connecting Principle.* (Princeton: Princeton University Press, Bollingen Series XX, 1973).

Koestler, Arthur. *The Roots of Coincidence.* (New York: Random House, 1972).

Kübler-Ross, Elisabeth. *On Death and Dying.* (New York: Macmillan, 1969).

Langley, Noel. *Edgar Cayce on Reincarnation.* (New York: Warner Books, 1967).

Martin, Joel, & Romanowski, Patricia. *We Don't Die: George Anderson's Conversations with the Other Side.* (New York: Berkley Books, 1989).

Mitchell, Edgar, ed. *Psychic Exploration.* (New York: G. P. Putnam's Sons, 1974).

Moody, Jr., M.D., Raymond A. *Life after Life.* (New York: Bantam Books, 1976).

Moody, Jr., M.D., Raymond A. *Reflections on Life after Life.* (Atlanta: Mockingbird Books, 1977).

Nadel, Ph.D., Laurie, with Haims, Judy, & Stempson, Robert. *Sixth Sense.* (New York: Avon Books, 1992).

Peat, F. David. *Synchronicity - The Bridge Between Matter and Mind.* (New York: Bantam Books, 1987).

Salk, Jonas. *Anatomy of Reality: Merging of Intuition and Reason.* (New York: Columbia University Press, 1983).

Stearn, Jess. *Edgar Cayce - The Sleeping Prophet.* (New York: Doubleday & Co., Inc., 1967).

Vaughan, Alan. *Incredible Coincidence - The Baffling World of Synchronicity.* (New York: Ballantine Books, 1989).

Vaughan, Alan. *Patterns of Prophecy.* (New York: Hawthorn, 1973).

Weiss, M.D., Brian L. *Many Lives, Many Masters.* (New York: A Fireside Book by Simon & Schuster, 1988).

# INDEX OF NAMES